T0077952

# WOMEN WHO TAKE YOUR BREATH AWAY

## THE LESLIE PETRONE STORY

JULIE TORRES-JOHNSON, Ph.D

**BALBOA.**PRESS
A DIVISION OF HAY HOUSE

Balboa Press books may be ordered through booksellers or by contacting:

Balboa Press
A Division of Hay House
1663 Liberty Drive
Bloomington, IN 47403
www.balboapress.com
844-682-1282

Because of the dynamic nature of the Internet, any web addresses or
links contained in this book may have changed since publication and
may no longer be valid. The views expressed in this work are solely those
of the author and do not necessarily reflect the views of the publisher,
and the publisher hereby disclaims any responsibility for them.

The author of this book does not dispense medical advice or prescribe the use
of any technique as a form of treatment for physical, emotional, or medical
problems without the advice of a physician, either directly or indirectly. The
intent of the author is only to offer information of a general nature to help
you in your quest for emotional and spiritual well-being. In the event you use
any of the information in this book for yourself, which is your constitutional
right, the author and the publisher assume no responsibility for your actions.

Any people depicted in stock imagery provided by Getty Images are
models, and such images are being used for illustrative purposes only.
Certain stock imagery © Getty Images.

Print information available on the last page.

ISBN: 978-1-9822-6736-0 (sc)
ISBN: 978-1-9822-6735-3 (e)

Balboa Press rev. date: 06/21/2021

# CONTENTS

*"There are no coincidences! I view accidents of chance as planned and premeditated gifts that I'm free to accept or reject."*

~Judith Knowlton~

# INTRODUCTION

My early life was riddled with accidents of chance that I refused to accept as premeditated gifts. Until one Sunday morning, my daughter Leslie interrupted my service with a call for help. That accident of chance became one of my greatest, planned and premeditated gifts.

Known to her friends as **"little"** because of her size, not her presence which was luminous, Leslie spread love wherever she went.

After a few months in ICU, while she was still strong enough to talk, Leslie reached out for my hand, looked deeply into my eyes, and whispered: *"Mom, promise me that after I'm gone, you will live your dream."*

That dream? To write a book about my extraordinary, one-of-a-kind daughter and our 50-year journey through the world of cystic fibrosis.

This is a story of love, discovery, growth, inspiration, pain, miracles and ultimately, transcendence.

*"If you look deeply into the palm of your hand, you will see your parents and all generations of your ancestors. You are the continuation of each of these people."*

~ Thich Nhat Hanh~

# CHAPTER 1

Leslie, who lived her life one day at a time, inherited her love of life from her dad's father, Grandpa Tony, who lived full out, without reservation. She had his wife, Grandma Josie, to thank for her strong life-force. Josie ran for an hour each day until she was 85 and lived with clarity of mind until her passing at age 94. No doubt this contributed to the fact that, at the time of her death, Leslie was the longest-ever female survivor of cystic fibrosis in California.

In addition to the qualities received from her paternal grandparents, Leslie inherited a strong, resilient spirit from my parents, Victor and Ramona. At the time of my birth, my father's physical disability made it impossible for him to work outside of the home. Consequently, he took care of the children while my mother, who barely earned enough to put food on the table for our family, worked as a seamstress in a New York City sweatshop.

Although Leslie's grandpa Victor had serious physical issues, like Leslie, he was able to rise above them. And, following in his footsteps, Leslie's only intoxication in life became a deep sense of love and duty for her family.

Her grandmother Ramona's contribution of resilience to Leslie came from her steady rise from seamstress to manager ("floor lady"), and, eventually, to owner of that sweatshop, which became a prosperous dress factory.

Ramona and Victor's legacy enabled Leslie to develop such a strong sense of self that, at the height of her disease, she was able to proclaim, "*I may have cystic fibrosis, but cystic fibrosis doesn't have me!*"

*"You are a child of the Universe, no less than the trees and the stars."*

~ Buddha~

# CHAPTER 2

The year was 1961. Leslie's father and I had just graduated from college together and were living in a one-bedroom apartment in Flushing, Long Island. I was teaching high school English, and Russell was working as a Sales Rep for Ortho Pharmaceutics when our daughter, Leslie Cathleen Petrone, drifted into our lives.

Her story began when I, a rather introverted teenager with little life experience, fell in love with her father, Russell Anthony Petrone. Despite being the only son of a minister, Russell had managed to squeeze as much life out of his otherwise dull, preacher's kid existence as was possible. To say that Russell had been around the block a few times would be an understatement.

Smoking was considered an unforgivable sin in his religion that believed, long before it was scientifically proven, that it caused lung cancer. So, when Russell, who was in his senior year of high school, was caught smoking, he was immediately expelled from his boarding school in Massachusetts and sent home to the upper Bronx in New York City.

Committed to having his son finish high school, his father enrolled him at The Greater New York Academy in Woodside, Long Island where, I was beginning my sophomore year.

You may recall the TV character, *"The Fonz,"* played by Henry Winkler, on the television show, "Happy Days." *"The Fonz,"* with his black hair combed back in a duck's tail, and his black leather jacket seemed like a replica of Russell Petrone during our high school days.

At eighteen, Russell was definitely more sophisticated than most of the students at my parochial high school. The scoop on him was that he was "too worldly," a term used to define someone who had stepped away from the narrow path of our religion.

Besides his charm and good looks, he was the only boy at my high school who had his own car, which was huge at the time. And, to top all of that, he had a part-time job after school which guaranteed that he had money to spend on his girlfriends.

As a fifteen-year-old serving as vice-president of the student council and dating its president, it had never even occurred to me that Russell would be romantically interested in me, or for that matter, that I could be enticed by his charm.

However, all it took was a ride in his car after school one day, and we were engaged by my seventeenth birthday and married a year later.

After years of trying to start a family, to no avail, Russell and I were overjoyed when we finally became pregnant. Surrounded by love and anticipation, it seemed like everyone around us—family, friends, the high school students I taught—were looking forward to the birth of Leslie Cathleen, our first child.

One day in May of 1961, while teaching my American literature class, I experienced one of the sweetest surprises of my life. I had just introduced "The Scarlet Letter," by Nathaniel Hawthorne to my students, when my classroom door suddenly flew open, and a sea of senior high school girls rushed in.

Two of them were carrying a large, beautifully decorated umbrella which they placed on the floor in the back of the classroom. After each girl had placed her gift under it, they all faced the front of the room where I stood with a shocked expression, and shouted, "**SURPRISE!**" And my first baby shower began.

I can still see those happy, excited faces interrupting my class to celebrate Leslie in vitro and her proud mother-to-be. And I shall always be grateful for the love and thoughtfulness that touched both Leslie's and my soul that day. In fact, I believe that Leslie's spirit responded in kind to all the love and thoughtfulness that we received because she never missed an opportunity to shower kindness and thoughtfulness on any of us.

From the very beginning, Leslie was a trusting baby who would jump into any arms that reached out for her. She laughed often and extended her joy to others. In fact, those qualities became her life-long hallmark.

At the same time, however, Leslie had health challenges that began in early infancy. She had trouble digesting her food, was plagued with diarrhea, and suffered from frequent bouts of bronchitis. As a toddler, she developed a voracious appetite that was difficult to quench, yet she never gained enough weight for her size.

Besides all of that, Leslie suffered from insomnia. So, her dad and I developed all kinds of schemes to get her to fall asleep. Her crib stood next to our bed in our one-bedroom apartment. So, her dad came up with the ingenious idea of tying a string from his big toe to Leslie's crib so he could rock her to sleep. And, there were many nights when, still rocking her crib, he fell asleep long before she did.

As a baby, Leslie loved riding in our Austin Healey. Car rides were the only thing that relaxed her enough to make her fall asleep. So, at night, we often drove around our neighborhood for hours, with Leslie lying on a pillow between the front seats, where the hum of the engine put her blissfully to sleep—and kept her asleep until we got home and carefully transferred her to the crib.

To say that Russell and I were sleep-deprived is an understatement. Leslie never took naps nor fell asleep before 10:00 pm. And since she started walking when she was only ten months old, she would climb out of her crib at the crack of dawn and wake us up. I knew better than to try to get a few winks after she appeared at our bedside because, if I didn't jump up immediately, she would go exploring either around the house or in the neighborhood.

Leslie, who was exceptionally small for her age, was the size of a normal, two-year-old when she was three. One morning, when she was three years old, she appeared at my bedside at 5:00 AM. I must have been extremely tired that morning because I closed my eyes again and fell sound asleep.

Instead of waking me up again as she usually did, Leslie, who was always hungry, simply wandered down the hall to the kitchen and reached up to the refrigerator handle. Once she managed to open the door, she crawled inside. Unable to open the sealed food containers, she dropped to the floor, opened the front door, stepped outside, and walked over to our neighbor's backyard.

Meanwhile, my neighbor, who had stepped out of his house for an early morning smoke, discovered Leslie standing beside his unfenced pool, petting his dog Smokie. Apprehensively, he walked toward her and said, *"Hi, Leslie, what are you doing here so early? Your mother must be looking for you."*

Since she knew him well, she simply said, *"I just came over to pet Smokie."* Although Smokie was enjoying the attention, our neighbor panicked about the unfenced pool directly behind her. So, trying not to startle her, he moved slowly in her direction and asked, *"Have you had your breakfast yet?"* When Leslie moved her little head from side to side, he said, *"Not yet? Then let's go home and get some."*

Meanwhile back home, when I opened my eyes and realized that I had fallen back asleep, I jumped out of bed calling her name. *"Leslie, Leslie honey, where are you?"* I ran to the kitchen, where I found the refrigerator door open and sealed containers of food all over the floor. *"She must be in the bathroom,"* I thought. Frantically calling her name, I ran down the hall toward the bathroom but before I got there, the doorbell rang. Anxious and crazed with foreboding, I turned toward the front door and opened it. And much to my surprise and relief, there was my little three-year-old looking as happy as ever in my perplexed neighbor's arms.

Because, for the first four 1/2 years of her life, Leslie had trouble digesting her food, she was not thriving. Concerned that, in spite of a voracious appetite, she gained very little weight and was much too small for her age, we treated her for every conceivable allergy on the planet. We took her off all dairy products, put her on soy formula, removed gluten, sugar, salt, and fat from her diet. Since nothing we tried seemed to make much of a difference, we simply decided to let her eat anything she wanted and do our best to help her enjoy life.

*"The dark night of the soul comes just before revelation. When everything is lost, and all seems like darkness, then comes the new life and all that is needed."*

~ Joseph Campbell~

# CHAPTER 3

Sadly, the stress caused by many sleepless nights, failed attempts at finding an adequate diet for Leslie, endless trips to the emergency room, the subsequent birth of her two brothers Rusty and Tommy, plus the demands of my full-time, teaching position had left Russell and me with very, little time to nurture our relationship.

So, even though we had been high school sweethearts, graduated from college together, and our college yearbook listed us as the couple most likely to succeed, our marriage ended in divorce when Leslie was four, Rusty was two, and Tommy was five months old.

Shortly after the upheaval of the divorce, I called Leslie's pediatrician to schedule a pre-kindergarten physical for her and discovered, much to my chagrin, that he was retiring. Although I didn't like having to change pediatricians in what seemed like the middle of the stream, I scheduled an appointment with the young doctor who was taking over the practice.

After examining Leslie and reviewing her medical history, the pediatrician asked if Leslie had ever been tested for cystic fibrosis: a chronic and often fatal, lung disease. When I admitted to never having heard of cystic fibrosis, the doctor handed me all kinds of information about the catastrophic condition and suggested that I take Leslie to Children's Hospital in Los Angeles, to be tested as soon as possible.

That night, as I lay in bed reading the literature the doctor had given me, I felt utterly overwhelmed. Although I was unfamiliar with cystic fibrosis, I realized that Leslie had several of the symptoms that were listed there. One passage, which clearly explained Leslie's frequent problem with diarrhea and her voracious appetite, stood out: *"the gastrointestinal tract and the pancreas become blocked, the absorption of fats and certain vitamins slows down, starving the body of essential nutrients…"*

For a fleeting moment, as I let the words sink in, my mind swirled with terrifying thoughts like: *"could this be what is happening to Leslie?"* Frightened by the very idea that my little girl could have such a devastating condition, I dismissed those troubling thoughts and put them out of my mind.

As the mother of three young children, taking a week off to go to Children's Hospital in Los Angeles was not going to be easy. Not only did I have to find a full-time babysitter for my 3-year-old and one-year-old toddlers, but I had to prepare a week's lesson plans for my American Literature and Advanced Spanish classes.

As it all turned out, finding a babysitter, making those lesson plans, and driving from Bakersfield to Los Angeles alone with Leslie, was the easiest part of the entire ordeal.

Leslie, who was extremely attached to me and to her brothers, had never spent a night away from her family. So, I knew that I had to make the trip as enticing as possible. As we packed our bags, and I talked about our upcoming adventure, Leslie asked, *"Mommy, are the boys coming to Los Angeles with us?"*

*"Leslie, this adventure is just for you and Mommy. Won't that be fun?"* I replied.

My daughter's next question was: *"Will you stay with me at the hospital?"* And of course, I assured her that I would. Although I had to move to a near-by, motel for the rest of the week, I did sleep in her room that first night. After that, I arrived at the hospital each day early enough to have breakfast with her and remained there until she fell asleep at night.

I had certainly dealt with dark nights of the soul before, but as I waited day after day to learn the outcome of Leslie's tests, I began to lose my conviction that they would prove her pediatrician wrong. It took three days to get all the results and, as time went on, feelings of fear and despair seemed to drape over me like a cold chill on a rainy night.

Each day, as I returned to her room, I would find my little extrovert busy telling some bed-ridden child a story or pushing a child in a wheelchair down the hall.

By the third day, Leslie had made friends with everyone on her floor. She knew the names of most of the patients, doctors, and nurses and everyone there seemed to know her as well. Just like it would one day be at Thornton Hospital in La Jolla, and the USC Medical & Transplant Center in Los Angeles, Leslie endeared herself to the doctors, respiratory therapists, nurses, and hospital staff.

Hearing stories about this compassionate, friendly, little girl even compelled her pediatrician to show up, every night in her room at bedtime, just to say good night.

After every conceivable test, the results were conclusive, and I was summoned to the pediatrician's office. Still, in a state of denial, I knocked on his door and waited for him to invite me in.

Before sitting down behind his large mahogany desk, the doctor offered me a chair. Noticing the anguished look on my face, the first thing he asked was, *"Do you have any family or friends with you here in Los Angeles?"* I told him that, although I had family back home in Bakersfield, I was alone in Los Angeles. Then he asked, *"Do you have anyone back home to lean on?"*

Instantly, my lifelong habit of never asking for help surfaced in my mind. And I inwardly asked myself the question, *"did I not ask for help because I really didn't believe that Leslie would be diagnosed with CF, or was it because of my own issues around believing that I didn't need anyone but myself?"* After all, I did have three sisters, and I was certain that one of them would have been willing to accompany me to Los Angeles. Yet, it had never occurred to me to ask one of them to be with me on this painful journey.

Feeling overwhelmed with a deep sense of emptiness, I found it difficult to speak up. With my head hung low, elbows resting on my knees and both hands on either side of my face, I shook my head from side to side. Then, choking back the tears, I answered the doctor's question with a very weak *"no."*

Unsure of the challenge ahead of me, I murmured almost under my breath, *"I'm hoping the tests were negative."* At that point, the pediatrician stepped from behind his large desk, pulled up a chair directly in front of me, and handed me the results of those dreaded tests. My first question after looking them over was, *"Is there a cure?"*

With great compassion, he took my hands in his and after a slight pause, said, *"Leslie has an advanced case of cystic fibrosis and there is no cure."*

*"An advanced case, and there is no cure?"* I whispered. Then, in a trembling voice I continued, *"how can that be possible!"* The doctor assured me that Leslie had been tested twice because the only visible sign of the disease was the clubbing: (a curving of the nails around the fingertips and toes.)

*"If everything goes well for her, maybe she'll make it to age seven,"* he continued. As we both walked toward the door, he put his hand on my shoulder and added, *"Take her home and make her happy and be sure and tell her teachers so that they will be especially kind to her."* Then he shook my hand and, as he opened the door for me, he said, *"it's all in God's hands now."*

In 1965, when Leslie was diagnosed with cystic fibrosis, neither her father nor I had ever heard of the mutated gene that both of us carried and had passed on to our child. So, as I walked out of the doctor's office that day, my initial reaction to that prognosis was disbelief. I refused to believe that my child could have such a horrific disease. *"No, No, No! I won't accept this! It can't be true!"* I uttered through trembling lips.

Feeling desperate to see Leslie and just hold her in my arms, I headed down the corridor toward her room. I opened the door, peeked in and noticed that she was not there. When the attending nurse told me that she was playing in another child's room, I actually felt grateful. I was not ready to face her. *"Thank God!"* I whispered under my breath as I hurried down the hall toward the elevator.

Once I reached the lobby, I headed directly for the front entrance and stepped outside. Paying no attention to the moving traffic, I ran across the street. The thought of losing my little girl had catapulted me into such a deep state of grief and depression that I lost all sense of reality.

So once on the other side of the street, totally unaware of anyone walking beside me, with no inhibitions left, I found myself crying out loud. Many strangers on the street that night, stopped and reached out to me, but as hard as they tried, none could dispel the agony that seemed to be tearing me apart. Still sobbing and emotionally out of control, I just hurried past them and continued walking from one street to another, until I reached a sidewalk that was teeming with homeless people. Wrapped in blankets trying to get through the cold, damp night, some were huddled together encircled by their shopping carts while others just sat outside of their cardboard houses.

Much too upset to feel any danger, I was circling my way around them when a homeless man sitting in front of his makeshift home, reached up, grabbed my hand, and offered to comfort me. *"Are you okay, Miss?"* he asked as he gently held my hand. Frightened by his spontaneous gesture, I instinctively pulled my hand away and ran past him.

The cold wind outside of me, and the fog of unhappiness inside were relentless. Trying to find some inner relief and ward off the chill of that damp, Los Angeles night that had me shivering, I wrapped my arms tightly around my upper body to no avail.

Alone in that dark and frightening place, the person I missed most at that moment of inconsolable grief, was my late father. In my delirium, I called out to him.

*"Papa! Papa! Please help me! What am I going to do? I can't just let my baby girl die."*

I really don't remember how I got through that dark night of the soul, but what I do remember is that, despite feeling totally desolate, I just kept on keeping on as I had always done. Freezing, mentally drained and physically exhausted, I managed to find my motel. I stumbled through the door of that dingy motel room and laid on the bed with my coat still on. And much too exhausted to move, I fell sound asleep for over an hour. Abruptly awakened by an altercation outside my door, I jumped out of bed, ripped off my clothes and stepped into the shower. The hot water running over my swollen face and down my weary back, relaxed me enough to pull myself somewhat together. And I returned to the hospital to see Leslie.

As usual, her pediatrician was in her room when I got there. Leslie, who never missed a detail when recapping her day, had his undivided attention. With absolutely no interruption on his part, he let her finish her story before saying, "*Guess what Leslie, you are going home tomorrow.*"

Thrilled with the prospect of seeing Rusty and Tommy again, Leslie enthusiastically replied, "*I can't wait to see my brothers. I have really missed them.*"

The pediatrician smiled warmly and said, "*I bet your brothers have missed you too.*" Then, as he always did, he kissed her on the forehead and said, "*Good night Leslie!*" But this time, before leaving her room, he turned to me and said, "*Good Luck!*"

Early the next morning, I gathered Leslie's things and prepared to take her home. As I was packing the car for our trip home, my mind wandered back to my childhood. And I remembered how my dad had turned around a prognosis of life-long paralysis due to his advanced case of rheumatoid arthritis.

After my birth, he had set his intention to live his life fully without a cane or a wheelchair. He did that for twenty-two years, until his untimely death, shortly after I graduated from college.

That memory filled me with the courage and hope that I could somehow turn this horrific prognosis around as well. Through his example, Papa had taught me to honor intentions and expect my dreams to come true.

At that moment, I had no idea how I was going to do that, but I set my intention for life rather than death for my little girl. And I decided that when we got home to Bakersfield, Leslie would get busy living, not dying.

All I wanted for her was that she would be able to live her life as normally as her brothers lived theirs. So, during that two-hour trip back to Bakersfield, I also decided that Leslie, her brothers, and I would learn from the past but live in the present moment, in an attitude of gratitude.

*"What we call obstacles are really the way the world's experience teaches us where we're stuck."*

~ Pema Chodron~

# CHAPTER 4

My mind was spinning as we drove back home to Bakersfield from Los Angeles. I knew I had to tell her about her disease, but I just could not come up with a way to do it without engendering fear in her. So, I decided to wait until we got back home where she felt safe and secure with her two, little brothers Rusty and Tommy. As it turned out, I never did find the right time to tell her.

Once we were home and settled in, I remembered the first thing the pediatrician had told me to do when I returned to Bakersfield: to purchase a portable oxygen tent where Leslie would spend hours each day.

Oxygen would be pumped into a plastic tent that was attached to the headboard of Leslie's bed and tucked under the mattress. Although the oxygen tent made it easier for Leslie to breathe, it also created an extremely uncomfortable, humid environment that she really disliked.

Her doctor had suggested that Leslie spend four hours in that oxygen tent when she got home from kindergarten each day. However, besides the damp feeling on her clothes and hair, she really hated spending all that time alone in the tent.

Leslie, who always had been able to talk me into anything, convinced me to allow her cousin Joann, who was like a sister to Leslie, to get into the tent with her. So, as soon as Joann entered the room, Leslie would invite her to get under the tent with her. Without hesitation, Joann would scramble to the middle of her bed to play with her Barbie dolls.

Since being in the tent was a wet, misty, uncomfortable experience, Joann could stay no longer than an hour at a time. And even in that short time, her hair and clothes got wet, and I would have to dry her and her doll's clothes before sending her home.

Although I tried to make an adventure out of the tent experience, nothing really helped to make it bearable for an extroverted five-year-old, even though she had trouble breathing outside of it.

Though I endeavored to make light of it, that oxygen tent still triggered a fear in Leslie of not being able to breathe, and of dying. And since I had still not found the courage to tell her about her disease, she kept asking questions: "*Mommy, am I in this tent because I'm going to die?"* Then she would follow that question up with heart-wrenching questions like, *"How does it feel to die? Does it hurt, Mommy?"* Despite my previous intention to take her home to live, it seemed like our discussions that first year, sadly, were more often about dying.

Nothing in life ever stays the same, however. Although I was at such a low point that I couldn't yet realize it, help was on the way.

*"Instead of being led by your problems. Be led by your dreams."*

~Ralph Waldo Emerson~

# CHAPTER 5

Struggling to cope with the horror of Leslie's diagnosis, I recalled a moment of great loss, some five years before Leslie was born. My beloved father had died in a horrific car accident. As I sat in a pew at his funeral, the voices rang out in unison, singing the familiar hymns that my dad and I had loved so much. On that day, however, the hymns brought little comfort. Feeling emotionally shattered and speechless, I just stared straight ahead at the bank of flowers on the altar.

Papa was the kind of father who, not only loved and guided me, but who always kept his word. He had taught me by example, to trust God whom he believed always kept His promises. So that questioning God's goodness as I was now doing, was totally foreign for me.

My mind was flooded with unanswered questions. Some of the most troubling were: *"where was God when Papa needed him?"* And, If God really was intimately tied to our human affairs, *"how could someone as faithful as Papa be the victim of such a horrific accident?"*

Very devoted to my religion for over twenty years, I had never questioned anything that I had been taught. However, after Papa's accident, I found myself dissecting everything that I had previously accepted with unwavering faith and I lost my faith in a caring, protecting God.

So, five years later, when I discovered that Leslie had cystic fibrosis and was not expected to live past the age of seven, that same troubling, unanswered question came up again. *How could a loving God whom I had devoutly, served my entire life, allow this to happen to my child?*

Convinced that the only way that Leslie could be saved from an untimely death was for me to stop questioning God's goodness, my mother, who loved Leslie and me very much, was relentless in begging me to change my perspective.

One day, when she was begging me to stop questioning God's goodness again, I became extremely angry and reeling with pain, I accused my mother of hitting me below the belt. "*Mama,*" I cried, "*do you mean to tell me that this God, whom I have served and loved all my life, is so vindictive that he would kill my child just to punish me?*"

Before she could answer, I screamed, *"If that is the kind of God I have been serving all my life, I want no part of him!"* Overwhelmed with guilt about, not only rejecting God, but disrespecting my mother, whom I had been taught to honor and obey under all circumstances, I ran out of the room.

From that time on, although the church had given me a warm sense of community and I had made lifetime friendships there, I never returned to the church of my childhood.

Moving from a place of unquestioning faith in God to the emptiness of not having anything to lean on, left me confused and frightened. Feeling like I was reaching up merely to touch bottom, I was consumed with the fear and depression that had dogged me since Leslie's diagnosis. Obsessed with the idea of losing Leslie, the oxygen tent intensified my anxiety. I was jumpy and unable to sleep at night. And by day, teaching and ordinary stresses, such as taking care of Leslie and my two toddlers, were becoming overwhelming.

Finally, I found a psychologist who promised to help me. In our first session, she suggested that I needed to find some way of sublimating my fear of losing Leslie into something that was very meaningful for me. However, after several sessions, nothing particularly helpful seemed to surface.

That is, until one day I mentioned that, as a child, I had loved school more than anything else in my life. I also told her that September, which marked the beginning of each school year, had always been my favorite month. The psychologist listened intently, then asked me if I had ever considered going to graduate school. Without pause or hesitation, I excitedly jumped up out of my chair and shouted, *"YES!"*

Thrilled to see me get excited about something, she asked what I planned to study there. For the first time in my adult life, I shared my lifelong dream of teaching Spanish at the college level. Knowing that school had been a means of escape from a rather dull childhood for me, the psychologist jumped on that.

Excited about having found a solution to my situational depression, she asked me what language I was interested in learning. With a smile on my face and an enthusiasm that she had never witnessed in me, I replied, *"since I am already fluent in Spanish, I want to learn French."*

After that session, I registered for a French class at the local college where a chance meeting with a man became a premeditated gift that forever changed Leslie's life and mine.

*"Nothing has ever happened or can happen to you that is not a gift and a blessing, but it's difficult to be thankful until you find the hidden benefit in what may seem at first to be a negative event."*

~ Dr. John DeMartini~

# CHAPTER 6

On the first day of that conversational, French class, the professor asked each of us to pick a partner. As I stood up and began searching the room, I approached a tall, thin man, wearing a blue sweater with a white shirt peeking out from under it. I introduced myself and asked him if he was interested in becoming my conversational French partner for the semester. He shook his head in agreement and said, *"I'm Loren Johnson."*

After practicing French together for a few months, we became good friends. One sunny day, as we were walking out of class, he startled me by asking a very personal question: *"Why is it,"* he asked, *"that such a beautiful woman never smiles?"*

*"Have you got an hour?"* I replied in a very sarcastic tone. *"Yes,"* he answered, *"as a matter of fact I do. How about having coffee after class tomorrow?"*

The next day after class, we met for coffee and I told him about Leslie, about my mother telling me that God was punishing me for questioning his goodness, and was taking my child from me. Then I confessed that my kids and tranquilizers were the only things that were keeping me from jumping off a bridge.

He listened patiently, without interruption. Then he said, *"And what have you decided to do about your little girl? Are you just going to let her die?"*

*"Of course, I don't want to let her die, but there doesn't seem to be anything I can do about it,"* I answered defensively.

*"Yes, there is something you can do about it,"* he calmly responded. *"You can turn to God for help."*

*TURN TO GOD FOR HELP?"* I shouted. Loren's comment had taken me back to my my mom's favorite Bible verses (*"God cannot be mocked,"* and *"The sins of the fathers are visited unto the children for the third and fourth generations."*) Feeling betrayed, I replied in a rather loud voice, *"IF YOU MEAN PRAYER, FORGET IT, I AM NOT SURE I EVEN BELIEVE IN GOD ANYMORE!"*

Noticing how references to God and the Bible had upset me, he changed his approach. *"My mother is a practitioner,"* he said, *"and I know she can help Leslie."* At that point in the conversation, the only words that really got my attention were, ***"I know she can help Leslie."***

*"What is a practitioner, and how can she help Leslie?"* I asked.

Loren replied with a question. *"Have you ever heard of metaphysics?"*

I remembered reading books written by Ralph Waldo Emerson, Walt Whitman, Henry David Thoreau, Thomas Paine, and other early transcendentalists. But all I could remember about them at the time, was that they were humanists who espoused the idea of the German Romantics about looking within rather than looking outside of oneself for answers to spiritual questions.

Although I was not even sure if my definition was correct, that was the extent of my knowledge of metaphysics. And I certainly could not understand how that knowledge could possibly help Leslie's disease or lift me out of the dark hole I was swimming in.

After that conversation, Loren and I had coffee after class on a regular basis. And during those coffee breaks, we did a lot of philosophizing: something I always loved to do. Obsessed with the idea of saving Leslie from an untimely death, I tossed and turned all night counting the hours until our next session.

Eventually, Loren introduced me to his mother, Alice Johnson who, not only became my Spiritual mentor, but engaged me in a cognitive restructuring process that revolutionized my thinking.

Although my father had already introduced me to the power of intention, Alice's spiritual guidance opened me to the healing power of unconditional love: something I had never personally experienced.

Since Alice knew that it was impossible to give to others what we didn't possess ourselves, she explained that, if I was to help Leslie, I had to begin seeing God and the world from a different perspective. At that crucial crossroads, Alice assured me that by changing my perception, I had the power to change anything about myself, my life—and, yes, even Leslie's prognosis.

*"Dear,"* she would say to me, *"you don't attract what you want, you only attract what you are."* At that time, the idea of (*"attracting what you are"*) was deeply troubling to me because I was a fearful, angry, bitter woman. And I certainly did not want to attract more of that.

From that point forward, all of Alice's efforts were spent in helping me to change the way I perceived my world. She helped me to understand that if I wanted to attract more love, more joy, and, as impossible as it then seemed, wholeness for Leslie, my approach to life had to become more positive.

Alice also taught me that distorted perceptions of God would make me vulnerable to the distorted perceptions of others. Therefore, I had to change my view of God as angry, punishing and vengeful to a loving presence that lived in me.

As Alice worked on my cognitive restructuring, she would say, *"My dear, since God is love, and fear cannot dwell in LOVE'S presence, your thoughts and words must extend only love."* What she said next stopped me in my tracks. *"Whenever we speak or act,"* she said, *"we are either extending love or multiplying fear."*

In describing my mind, she often used the analogy of a light bulb. The light was already there and all I had to do was turn it on. And since, according to Alice, love and fear were mutually exclusive, the way I turned on the light was to eliminate fear from my thinking. So, each time she saw me she would ask, *"Julie, did you extend love or multiply fear today?"*

To help me keep that light turned on, Alice taught me that negative words like "hate" came from fear.

Therefore, whenever I would say how much I hated Leslie's disease, she would simply look me in the eye and say, *"My dear, you don't hate anything. "Hate,"* she would say, *"comes from fear and as long fear is present in you, God's unconditional love cannot do its perfect, healing work in you or Leslie."*

After a lifetime of multiplying fear rather than extending love, I must admit that it did take a while to literally change my perspective. However, I eventually became vigilant enough to notice words that were multiplying fear, and began replacing them with words and actions that extended only love and healing.

Something Alice said often was, *"Love is reflected in love!"* When I asked her what that meant, she said that if I raised my consciousness to the energy of love, every possibility in the present and future would exist timelessly for me. So, my first action step in this process was to become aware of my fearful thoughts and words as often as possible, and before acting on them, raise them up to the power of unconditional love.

With Alice's continuing guidance, I stopped thinking of God as angry or punishing and began, instead, to perceive God as an expression of healing love that lived in me and in Leslie. That meant that I needed not only to see myself as already healed and whole, but I had to visualize Leslie the same way.

According to Alice, giving and receiving were the same. Therefore, all the love that I was giving to Leslie, her brothers and my students was automatically returning to me.

As I listened to what Alice was saying, I thought how that principle was so readily apparent in nature, where countless organisms breathe in carbon dioxide and breathe out oxygen for us, while we breathe in that oxygen and breathe out carbon dioxide for them.

Setting my intention on finding wholeness for Leslie, I not only expected it, but committed to whatever action was necessary to help make that happen. Since I learned that the present is the only place where miracles are possible, I tried my best to live each day in the present.

In order to help convince myself that remission was possible for Leslie, I began to read stories about spontaneous remissions. I read Bible stories about Jesus' healing ministry. I read about people who had replaced fear with love and had experienced the healing power of love in all sorts of physical challenges. Those stories strengthened my conviction that it was possible to stop the destructive effects of cystic fibrosis in Leslie's body.

My next challenge was to confront every parent's greatest nightmare: the fear of outliving one's children. Remembering how doctors had given up on my father when he decided to do the impossible, I decided that even though doctors had given up on Leslie, I hadn't and I wouldn't.

I claimed grace by affirming one of my favorite Bible verses, *"by Grace I live and by Grace, I am released."* Then, before I fell asleep at night, I would say, *"Leslie, by Grace you live and by Grace you are released from cystic fibrosis."* And since affirming grace seemed to move me into an attitude of gratitude, I found myself feeling more and more grateful for everything and everyone in my life including the circumstances in which I presently found myself.

However, one of the most difficult concepts I grappled with while in this process of cognitive restructuring was to see only wholeness in Leslie. In fact, I had to see Leslie as being no different than her two healthy brothers. This was certainly not easy. Leslie, at age five, not only had to spend time in a portable oxygen tent but was also developing rheumatic fever.

As difficult as this transition was, I recognized that my fear thoughts, though still present, were dissipating enough for me to begin believing that a spontaneous remission, which medical authorities claimed was impossible with gene-based diseases, was possible for Leslie.

Although I had done lots of work on myself, I was not aware of the small, internal shifts that had already taken place in me and given me the needed courage to take that huge, final step. I had always thought of new beginnings in terms of large *external* changes. But I had learned through this process, that it was those small, unrecognizable, *internal* shifts that had prepared me to do what I was called to do now.

So, instead of focusing on what my precious girl could not do, I began to imagine what she was capable of doing. And although I knew that the voice of fear would try to convince me to play small, I decided to play BIG. And with Alice's guidance, I embarked on a journey that forever transformed Leslie's life and mine.

*"The greatest gift you have to give is that of your own self-transformation."*

~Lao Tzu~

# CHAPTER 7

My first task in helping Leslie to see herself as whole was to free her from the oxygen tent, where she was currently spending four hours each day. I had done a thorough job of convincing her how sick she really was, and how necessary the oxygen tent was, so trying to undo all of that was not going to be a cakewalk. Difficult as it seemed, I was ready to engage in the lengthy process of helping my little girl to see herself differently.

I had discussed my plan to wean Leslie off the oxygen tent with her father, with whom I had a generally amicable relationship. In this case, however, Russell and I sharply disagreed. He was adamantly opposed to removing the oxygen tent. His concern based on the fear of losing his little girl, resonated deeply in my heart. And I asked myself, *"Are you aware of what you have gotten yourself into? Julie, are you in over your head?"*

And yet, since I believed that remission was possible for Leslie, I persevered. Since I wanted to teach her some of the beliefs and concepts that I had learned, I began by telling her how strong she was, and that she was no different than her healthy brothers. I explained to her that, even though the oxygen tent had helped her in the past, she no longer needed it.

At first, Leslie was understandably very fearful of leaving the oxygen tent behind. If I tried to assure her that she could breathe without it, she would just smile and then assure me that she could not. Sometimes, I even asked her if she wanted to try breathing without the oxygen tent for a day, and her reply would always be, *"No thank you mommy!"*

This went on for months. The day came, however, when Leslie asked me if I believed that she could breathe without the oxygen tent. Without hesitation, I enthusiastically said *"YES!"* Then she looked at me and said, *"Maybe I can, but I don't want to try."*

The bottom line was, that before I could take her out of that oxygen tent, we both had to believe, without the slightest tinge of doubt, that she could survive without it. In other words, if we jumped ship together, I had to be sure that Leslie would not drown.

Finally, after a year of hard work, the day came when I felt that both Leslie and I were ready to take that big step toward remission. Alice had assured me that if taking her out of the tent created a sense of panic in Leslie or in me, I was to simply hold her hand, and calmly reassure her that I would put her back into the oxygen tent if either of us felt that she needed it.

Once we decided to leave the tent behind, neither of us got much sleep for the first three weeks. I would lie next to her in her bed, with her little hand in mine, affirming and holding the thought of wholeness for her. With unwavering faith in God's perfect plan for her life, I kept assuring her that never for a single instant does the healing spirit of God's unconditional love cease its perfect action.

As I held that thought and prayed with her night after night, I felt the presence of God's healing love flowing as perfect wholeness through me, and through Leslie's little body.

Sometimes, when she was coughing a lot, she would suggest that perhaps I should put her back into the oxygen tent. Holding her little hand in mine, I would softly say, *"Leslie Honey, you are strong and healthy like your brothers. You are not sick. Only sick children need to be in oxygen tents."*

Then I would ask her, *"Do your brothers live in oxygen tents?"* *"No"* she would say, *"because they are not sick!"*

*"Neither are you,"* I countered.

Then I would repeat a powerful prayer until she fell asleep. Sometimes, I would repeat that prayer for hours, until the coughing had stopped, and she was breathing normally.

To make the prayer more understandable for a small child, I personalized it. *"God is Spirit,"* I would quietly but reverently say to her. *"and Leslie, you are God's image and likeness. Therefore, Leslie honey, although you have a body, you are much more than your body. You are spiritual."*

On some level that neither of us understood at the time, the absolute truth that I was affirming lifted both her mind and mine to the spiritual level, where all healing occurs. Leslie never did return to the oxygen tent. And as her coughing subsided, she was able to sleep through the night without having me by her side.

Even with all that progress, I found it challenging not to run to her room every time I heard her cough during the night. Whenever I mentioned this to

Alice, she would simply say, *"My dear, do you run to the boys every time you hear them cough during the night?"*

*"The answer to that question,"* I said to her, *"is a resounding NO! I do not run to Rusty and Tommy's room when I hear them cough at night. But then, Leslie has cystic fibrosis, and her brothers are perfectly healthy. Leslie takes over twenty pills a day, she takes digestive enzymes before each meal. She needs to have her chest pounded every day. She is never allowed to play outdoors with her brothers if the weather is cold, windy, or if it is raining or snowing."*

Alice listened without interruption and then she said, *"I know it sounds impossible, my dear, but with God's help, you will be able to bridge that gap."* Although she didn't say it, I knew she meant that even though I had come a long way, I still had a very long way to go. So, I persevered.

Life was now different from that first year, when I confronted the fear of losing her every day. Leslie never returned to the oxygen tent. Her coughing subsided tremendously and she eventually stopped coughing altogether.

Her brothers and I lived our lives in the present moment, where all healing occurs. Instead of bringing the past into the present like we had been accustomed to doing, we now reached for the infinite possibilities of the future and never put off anything for tomorrow that could be enjoyed that day.

The commitment I had made on our way home from Children's Hospital two years earlier came to pass. Instead of dying at the age of seven as her prognosis had predicted, Leslie experienced a spontaneous remission, two months before her 8th birthday, that stopped all the effects of cystic fibrosis for almost ten years.

*"To dare is to lose one's footing momentarily. To not dare is to lose oneself."*

*~ Soren Kierkegaard~*

# CHAPTER 8

Although Leslie was doing very well in remission, everyone in Bakersfield was still expecting her to die. Our extended family, her pediatrician, her teachers were all catering to her because they didn't expect her to make it to third grade.

With input from Alice Johnson, I determined that it would be best to move my family to another location where Leslie would no longer be a victim of others' "death thoughts." We needed a fresh start.

The idea of moving was frightening because I had no idea of where I could go. I had a tenured teaching position at a time when tenure was difficult to get. Besides, on Monday afternoons, I was learning French in graduate school and loved it.

Tommy was three, Rusty was five, and Leslie, who was seven, was just finishing second grade. I knew that if I were going to move out of Bakersfield, it had to be before September.

Meanwhile, my friendship with Loren Johnson had continued. I was passionately grateful that he had introduced me to metaphysics and to his mother, Alice, who had helped to save Leslie from an untimely death.

Loren had just received a fully paid scholarship to a doctoral program in math at The University of Arizona, in Tucson. When I shared my dream of becoming a Spanish professor, he encouraged me to apply to The University of Arizona's four-year doctoral program in Spanish.

I applied and received a four-year, fully paid scholarship to the doctoral program. The acceptance letter from The University of Arizona seemed like a sure sign that Spirit was preparing the way for a new beginning for all of us, especially for Leslie. So, I finished my French class, resigned from my tenured teaching position, left my family of origin and my lovely home behind, and moved with Loren and the kids to a small apartment near campus.

After our first year in Tucson, Loren and I were married, and he adopted my children. Although I was not passionately in love with him at the time, we had a lot in common. We loved to read, and as two intellectuals excelling at our full-time doctoral programs, we often engaged in meaningful activities and conversations.

We spent a lot of time together as a family, too, playing games, camping on weekends, and attending a Unity church. Those first two years of marriage to Loren not only exponentially increased the quality of my children's lives; but were two of the best years of my own life so far.

Besides becoming a very close-knit family, Loren and I finished the master's track of our doctoral programs with flying colors. In the fall, when we would begin our doctoral tracks, I was really looking forward to becoming a teaching assistant. Leslie and her two brothers were doing well in their new schools and had made some good friends.

I felt extremely grateful for the emotional stability that my new marriage had created for Leslie, Rusty, and Tommy. She and the boys loved their new stepfather, and they were all thriving. And, at the time, that was all that really mattered to me.

But suddenly, everything changed. Loren, running out of funds for child support for his three daughters from a previous marriage, began a job search and accepted a job as an actuary in Hartford, Connecticut, without my knowledge.

I was stunned and angry. The question I kept asking myself was, *"How could he leave his doctoral program at this point—and expect me to leave mine? How could we uproot the children, who have established friendships and are doing so well?"*

I felt disillusioned with my marriage, and bereft of the life we had all previously enjoyed in Tucson. Yet, knowing that the children loved Loren and that I had promised that he could make all financial and family decisions in our marriage, we packed up and moved to Connecticut.

And, despite the objections of my advisor who assured me that I was making a big mistake, I walked away from the last two years of my lifelong dream of becoming a Spanish professor.

The move to Connecticut began a nomadic period for our family. Loren always managed to find wonderful positions but, just as quickly, he would become bored and change jobs. During our six years in Connecticut, we moved to three different towns.

Then, Loren got a fabulous position as the math coordinator for The American School in Barcelona, one of the most prestigious schools in Spain.

Unfortunately for me, there were no job openings at the high school level. So, I became Rusty's 4th-grade teacher, which made him, Leslie and Tommy extremely popular on campus.

Barcelona turned out to be a wonderful place for all of us. It was especially good for Leslie, who, now eleven years old and in sixth grade, was still very much in remission. In fact, during that year in Barcelona, Leslie passed her school physical with flying colors and required no more medical attention than her brothers.

Rusty and Tommy meant everything to Leslie, almost from the moment each of them was born. Wise beyond her years, their big sister nurtured, encouraged, scolded and protected them. Nothing illustrates this better than what we fondly call "the soccer story."

There was a large park across the street from our apartment. One day, we noticed a soccer game in progress there. Since none of us knew anything about soccer, we found a large bench and sat down to watch our first game. As we became absorbed in what was going on, I noticed how intently Rusty seemed to be concentrating on the game.

Although at that time Rusty didn't know a single word of Spanish, he was listening with an intensity that I had never before noticed in my nine-year-old. It didn't take him long to figure out that the Spanish word for "*ball*" was "*pelota*," and that the Spanish word for "*here*" was "*aqui*."

After watching for about twenty minutes, Rusty suddenly jumped up and pointing to his outstretched hand, began shouting, "HEY, PELOTA AQUI! AQUI! HEY, PELOTA AQUI!"

At first, the teenage boys seemed to ignore him. "*Those boys don't want you in their game,*" scolded his eleven-year-old sister. Then, in the authoritative voice that she often used with her little brothers, she said, "*Rusty, sit down and watch the game with the rest of your family!*"

Totally ignoring Leslie's command as he often did, Rusty stood right where he was planted. With that grin on his face that Leslie would years later, grow to love each time he entered her hospital room with his renown, home made, turkey soup, he continued to shout out to those boys. Just in case the soccer players had not heard him the first time, running toward the team, he shouted a little louder "HEY,

PELOTA AQUI, PELOTA AQUI!, PELOTA AQUI!!"

The soccer team stopped their game for a minute and went into a huddle. Then with a big smile on his face, the captain said something to the others in Catalan, a native language spoken in Barcelona that we didn't understand. Since most of the team smiled as they looked toward Rusty, it seemed to Leslie that they were making fun of her little brother. She wasn't about to tolerate that! So, she stood up again, and with an even stronger sense of older-sister authority, shouted, *"RUSTY GET OVER HERE! Can't you see he's telling his team to ignore you?"*

At that point, agreeing with Leslie, I was about to insist that Rusty join us on the bench when the teenager holding the soccer ball looked our way, smiled and passed the ball to him. With a proud grin on his face, Rusty, not only received the ball, but was in the game for the duration.

Shocked, yet impressed by her little brother's tenacity, Leslie smiled, looked around at the crowd, and shouted, *"THAT'S MY BROTHER!"*

After a marvelous year in Barcelona, I became pregnant with our fourth child, and we decided to give birth to Eric in the USA. As usual, Loren found a wonderful job.

This time, he was to be the Math Coordinator in a large school district in Windsor, Connecticut.

Since Eric was born in the middle of September, for the first time in my teaching career, I took six months off and became a stay-at-home mom. Those six months were wonderful not only for me and the baby, but for Leslie. She had fallen in love with Eric, and could hardly wait to get home after school to hold him.

Although I knew Loren had no intention of permanently giving up our nomadic existence, I felt that Eric's birth ushered in a need for more stability. So, I insisted on settling down in one place and purchasing a home of our own. Consequently, when Eric was only six months old, I went back to full-time teaching at the local high school, and we purchased a lovely home in Coventry, Connecticut.

Although we had some relationship issues, our marriage seemed strong enough. We had dinner together as a family every evening, attended church each week, and camped a great deal. I even enrolled in a doctoral program in psychology at the University of Connecticut.

Leslie loved her new life in Connecticut. Being the homebody that she always was, living in a permanent home of her own seemed to give her a greater sense of emotional security. Incredibly creative, she spent endless hours decorating her bedroom and helping Russ and Tom cozy-up their space as well.

Just like any other typical girl, Leslie attended Girl Scout meetings, camp-out weekends, and summer camp. In high school, she lived the same normal, sports-oriented life that her two brothers experienced. Inspired by her brother Russ, who was actively involved in track, she became a long-distance runner. All during this period, Leslie continued to be healthy. She never coughed, and hardly ever got a cold.

Despite the mutated cystic fibrosis gene that kept the chloride ions from moving perfectly in her body, her lung secretions did not become thick and congested, so she never got pneumonia. Without taking enzymes, her gastrointestinal tract and pancreas seemed to absorb fats and break down her food so perfectly that, as a fifteen-year-old who was 5'4", she maintained the very normal weight of 114 lbs.

All of us seemed to be content—except for Loren who missed our nomadic existence. Once again disenchanted with his job, he began finding distractions away from home.

Despite the many moves for our family during our ten years together, I had convinced myself that giving my husband complete control meant that the family and I would enjoy a lifetime of love and security. However, the problem with giving any person that much power is that eventually, someone will stand against it. And in this case, Leslie, now a teenager with a strong sense of self, was the only one of us who dared to do that.

*"Just do as your father says,"* I would beg. But as a teenager claiming her sense of independence, she continued to question Loren's arbitrary decisions, something that none of us had ever done.

Trying to make Loren understand that unquestioning obedience would not work with a teenager, I would plead with him to be more understanding, to be more objective.

Questioning his authority made him so resentful and distant, that he began coming home later and later from work. Although I was aware that Loren was becoming bored with me and our marriage, my gratitude for Leslie's wholeness, the thrill of having a healthy baby and a home of our own, kept me in a state of absolute denial. And for the sake of Leslie's emotional and physical stability, I chose to pretend that everything was okay.

Yet, I knew that questioning his absolute authority and pushing for an egalitarian relationship would have repercussions. And, like so many women who try to pretend that they didn't know about the other woman, I knew long before he told me that he had found one.

*"You find peace, not by rearranging the circumstances of your life but by realizing who you are at the deepest level."*

~ Eckhart Tolle~

# CHAPTER 9

At this point, Leslie was still healthy and very, happy with her life in Coventry. Panicked at the thought of destabilizing her and her brother's lives, I was willing to do anything to make Loren want to stay with us. But, after a year of keeping his secrets, I was becoming as sick as my secrets.

Although I kept the details of our dysfunctional marriage from the children, once I opened the door to fear, it covered up the empowered woman that lived inside. And all the good decision-making skills that I had earlier so diligently modeled for Leslie and her brothers, were no longer apparent.

A Course in Miracles says, *"You who perceive yourself as weak and frail, with futile hopes and devastated dreams, born but to die and suffer pain, there is nothing you cannot do."*

I wanted to perceive myself as strong once again because it was going to take strength to tell Leslie and her brothers about the divorce, and especially that we had to move out of our beautiful, new house.

I had done such a good job of hiding our marital issues from the children that, when I announced the divorce, Leslie, feeling blind-sided, turned her full rage on me. *"Why are you doing this, Mom?* she cried. *"We have such a wonderful family."* Then, seeing the divorce as a personal attack, she ran out of the room screaming, *"Why are you doing this to me?"*

Once the house was sold, Leslie and Eric moved into a two-bedroom apartment with me, and Russ and Tom moved in with their dad. Leslie, now sixteen, was so unhappy about the situation that she had one meltdown after another. During one especially intense quarrel, she furiously accused me of ruining her life, and stormed out of the room.

Although we had had mother-daughter arguments in the past, we had never had a confrontation like that one. So, I waited a couple of hours before knocking on her door and asking her if we could talk. Much to my surprise, instead of demanding that I get out of her room and leave her alone, she opened her door and let me in.

I sat on her bed, put my arm around her and told her how much I loved her. Still angry with me, instead of saying, "I love you too, Mom," as she usually did, she just went on and on about the emotional pain the divorce had caused her. Sobbing uncontrollably, she mumbled that she simply could not get over the pain she was feeling about splitting up our family, leaving our new house, and having to change her lifestyle.

At that point, I realized that the time had come to tell her the truth about why her dad and I had divorced. I began by telling her how much her dad loved her and her brothers and that the divorce had had nothing to do with them. As calmly as possible, I simply told her that her dad had fallen out of love with me, and had fallen in love with someone else. My candor touched her so deeply, that she wrapped her arms around me, and we both cried for a long time.

As we sat there crying and feeling each other's pain, I sobbed, *"Leslie honey, I promise you that one day, Russ and Tom will be with us again, and we will all live together in an even nicer house than the one we just left in Coventry."*

Although neither of us knew how we would live out that promise, it seemed like the only thing that could bring any comfort to her grieving heart that day. When we had finally talked it out, I kissed her and said, "I love you, Leslie honey." As I was walking out the door, I heard her say, "I love you too, Mom."

Though my relationship with Leslie was less strained after that conversation, the changes in our lives, especially separating from Russ and Tom, were having a devastating effect on her. So, I called my sister Becky in California. Becky, who was a teenager when I was born, had always been like a mother than older sister to me, and a very dear auntie to Leslie.

As always, my sister was a comforting presence that made it easy for me to share my concerns about Leslie, who was having much more difficulty dealing with the divorce than her brothers. Saddened that I had carried this awful burden alone for so long, Becky said, *"Julie, I want you and the kids to come home to your family in California. We love you and want you here."*

"HOME?" I cried. *"I am at home."*

*"No!"* Replied Becky. *"You're not home anymore. Home is where you are loved and supported. This is your home now. This is where Leslie, the boys, and you belong."*

Desperately searching for answers, I asked, *"Where would we live?"* Knowing that my car broke down a lot, I asked, *"How would we get there?"* I followed-up that question with, *"where would I work? I am the sole support of my family now, and I hear there are no teaching jobs in California."*

*"Just get in your car and head for California,"* said Becky. *"I'll find a place to live for you and the kids. We will even find you a teaching job. You just need to get here.* Then with the warmth that only sister Becky seemed to be capable of, she added*: "Julie, will you please just come home!"*

Her voice was so soothing and reassuring that as soon as I hung up, I knew that Bakersfield, California was where the kids and I needed to be. So, I told them that we would be moving back to California at the end of the school year.

Her brothers seemed okay with the move, but Leslie was adamant that she was not going to leave her school and friends in Connecticut. So, to keep her feeling as happy and emotionally stable as possible, I made some arrangements for her to stay in Coventry with her best friend's family and finish high school there.

My next step was to meet with my principal and tell him that as soon as the school year ended, I planned to quit my tenured teaching position in

Coventry and move the family back to Bakersfield, California.

Shocked at the news, he was quick to inform me about the shortage of teaching jobs there. *"Julie,"* he said, *"There is a teacher shortage in California. You are making a big mistake. You have a stable, tenured teaching position here. It would be very irresponsible of you to move your family to the uncertainty of California."*

From a rational point of view, I knew he was right. So, I listened respectfully, thanked him for his advice, and assured him that I would think about it. However, needing the love and warmth of a family more than I needed the security of a stable teaching position, at the end of the school year, I resigned and headed for California with Russ, Tom and Eric. While Leslie, who was still healthy and strong, moved in with her friend's family.

After we had settled into the furnished, two-bedroom condo that Becky had waiting for us, I applied to the local school district. And during my third interview for the only teaching job available in my field, I just happened to mention that while in graduate school, I had studied French: something that would make all the difference a year later.

As it turned out, the teaching district was desperately in need of an Advanced Spanish teacher who was also credentialed to teach American and English literature. My master's degree in Spanish, from The University of Arizona, got me the job. Best of all, I would be earning much more than I had earned in Connecticut.

Although I loved my teaching job, that first year was not easy for the boys nor for me. My car kept breaking down and living in a 1000sq foot, two-bedroom condo with two teenage boys and a three-year-old was difficult at best.

To make matters even more complicated, three months after we had moved to California, Leslie decided that she simply couldn't live without her family, and returned to California to share my bedroom in that small condo.

Although Leslie was happy to be with her family in California, she continued to have meltdowns about our living arrangements. One day, about six months after Leslie had arrived, I heard her cough. Assuming she was just getting a cold, I handed her some cough drops and put it out of my mind.

A few weeks later, I was in the kitchen preparing a cup of coffee when Leslie entered the room with her hand over her mouth trying to cover her cough. Soon, she began to cough uncontrollably. I looked over to where she was standing and asked, *"Leslie honey, do you still have that cold?"*

*"I feel alright,"* she answered. *"I just can't get over this cough."* As she said that, I felt an unusual tightness in my throat and a hot pain in my gut. Although It had been almost ten years, I thought I recognized the horrific sound of the cystic fibrosis cough. Knowing how stressed and anxious she had been over the divorce, a very painful question came to mind: *"Could Leslie be coming out of remission?*

The thought that Leslie, who was soon to be seventeen, might be coming out of remission was almost impossible for me to accept. Unable to cope with it, I pushed it down, deep inside just as I had done with all my pain.

The divorce, being totally, financially responsible for four kids, Leslie's cough, and the sibling rivalry in those tight quarters had taken a terrible toll on me. And despite all that Alice had taught me about the power of words to create my life, I began using self-deprecating humor as a coping mechanism.

*"Challenges are gifts that force us to search for a new center of gravity. Don't fight them. Just find a new way to stand."*

~ Oprah Winfrey~

# CHAPTER 10

One day, in the teacher's lounge, I was telling a story of my life in that small, two-bedroom condo with my four children. When I had everyone's attention, I told them I had come up with a good name for our living space. *"I'm calling our condo a snake pit,"* I said, *"because, at times, that is how it feels."*

The teachers roared with laughter. After that, every time I walked into the lounge, someone was sure to ask, *"Julie, do you have another snake pit story for us?"*

One day, as I was entertaining the teachers with another snake pit tale, I noticed that although most of the teachers were laughing, there was a teacher at the far end of the room who seemed to find no humor in my story.

I can still picture the compassionate expression on her face as she walked across the room, sat next to me, and whispered in my ear, *"Julie, have you ever tried meditation?"*

When I told her that I had not, she invited me to her meditation group. I was just about to decline when something inside of me nudged me to accept.

Everyone in the meditation group was sitting in a circle when I arrived. As soon as I took my place in the circle, I was asked to introduce myself. "*I'm Julie Johnson*," I began. "*I teach advanced Spanish, American, and English literature in the local high school. I'm the single parent of four lovely children and we all live in a two-bedroom condo. It feels very crowded and they fight a lot. My daughter Leslie still misses our home in Connecticut and complains a lot about our living arrangements here. Although she still seems healthy and strong, her constant cough frightens me. I fear that she might be coming out of a ten-year remission from cystic fibrosis. And other than praying, I don't know what to do about it.*"

At that point, my lips began to tremble, and I stopped to catch my breath. As I did that, the leader jumped in and asked, "*Julie, how does it feel to be wholly responsible for four children?*"

"*Once I saw a movie called Snake Pit, starring Olivia de Havilland,*" I replied. "*It was a story about a woman in a room full of snakes that were reaching up, trying to bite her. She kept trying to evade them but couldn't. That movie was so frightening to me that I never forgot it! Sometimes, my crowded condo feels like that. So, I call it a snake pit.*"

I laughed nervously, expecting them to laugh with me, but nobody did. It was a very awkward moment, to say the least. Neither the leader nor anyone else in the group found humor in any of it. Finally, the seemingly endless silence was broken by the group leader who said, *"Oh my dear, you have to change that affirmation."*

*"What affirmation?"* I asked.

*"My home is a snake pit!"* she replied.

*"I never thought of that statement as an affirmation,"* I countered.

Then, besides assuring me with absolute certainty that it was an affirmation, she talked about how our affirmations impact our lives. Suddenly, as I prepared to refute her words, Alice and all she had taught me years earlier about the power of words to create my destiny, came to mind. *"I know that!"* I thought. *"How could I have forgotten so quickly?"*

Now, like Alice so many years ago, that group leader was reminding me of the power of my words to create my reality. In a kind, gentle tone, she assured me that the more I called my home a snake pit, the more fear and and chaos I would experience there. *"My dear,"* she said in a tone that reminded me of Alice, *"let's change that affirmation to "My home is a haven of peace and joy."*

*"MY HOME IS A HAVEN OF PEACE AND JOY?"* I screamed. *"You have to be kidding!"* Then, feeling embarrassed for my spontaneous outburst, I became very silent for a few moments before breaking down into uncontrollable sobs. It was the first time I had allowed myself to cry without restraint since my painful divorce, and after so many years of remission, hearing Leslie cough again. Nobody in that group made the slightest attempt to comfort or stop me. Realizing that I really needed to release my pain, they just sat there silently and let me cry it out.

I must have sobbed for ten minutes before quieting down enough to allow the group leader to speak.

*"Julie,"* she said, *"your home may not seem like a haven of peace and joy right now, but I promise you, that if you change your affirmation to 'my home is a haven of peace and joy,' and meditate on it every day, your home will become exactly that."*

At that point, I realized that as much as Alice had taught me about the power of thought and the power of my words to create my reality, she had not taught me how to meditate. Thinking that, if it had been that important, Alice would have taught me how to do it, I began making excuses.

*"For starters,"* I said, *"I don't know how to do it. Besides, my home is much too noisy to try something like that. The truth is, that I simply don't have enough privacy."* Now on a roll, I began to point out all the time-constraints that would make a commitment to meditation impossible for me.

The group leader listened politely until I paused long enough for her to jump into the conversation. *"Julie,"* she asked, *"would you like to learn how to meditate?"* When I finally agreed that it could be a good idea, she followed up that question by saying, *"If you come to our group each week, you will learn how."* Then she caught me off guard by changing the subject and asking, *"At what time do you get up each day?"*

I began by saying, *"believe it or not, although I have to get up at 5:30 each morning, I'm not a morning person."* Then I told her that, in order to have enough time to run six miles each morning, make breakfast and lunch for the kids, and drive Eric to his babysitter before showing up for my 8:00 AM class at the local high school, I had to get up at 5:30 AM.

As if she had not heard my last statement, the group leader suggested that I arise at 5:00 AM and begin practicing my new affirmation and meditation technique.

Convinced that she had not heard me, I repeated that, not being a morning person, getting up any earlier than 5:30 AM was impossible.

At that point, she invited me to stop talking and experience ten minutes of meditation with the group. As I closed my eyes, I felt like I had been dipped into the same warm pool of peace and contentment that I had experienced long before the divorce and all its ramifications.

When I finally opened my eyes, the group leader assured me that meditation was a way of raising my vibration to the power of Love where healing is possible. Remembering how I had helped to co-create a spontaneous remission for Leslie when she was seven, that day, I set my intention to doing whatever was necessary to change my chaotic mind to one of absolute peace again.

Besides attending the meditation group at 7:00 PM every Thursday night, I arose at 5:00 AM every morning, sat quietly in my living room and affirmed, *"My home is a haven of peace and joy!"* Then, I sat quietly for thirty minutes.

At first, those thirty minutes seemed like a lifetime. My thoughts would wander to everything but the affirmation. Sometimes, when I couldn't slow my monkey mind down, I simply repeated the affirmation again and again until the timer went off.

However, I soon found that as I honored my commitment morning after morning, the thirty minutes seemed to pass by more quickly each day. And after six months, I really looked forward to it.

As the group leader had promised, once I found the peace of God for myself again, my children found it too, and our home became a haven of peace and joy.

*"You create your reality with your intentions."*

~ Gary Zukav~

# CHAPTER 11

At the end of my first year of teaching in Bakersfield, there were more cutbacks, and since I was one of the last teachers who was hired a year earlier, I received a pink slip: a devastating set-back.

I loved my job, and especially loved living near my family of origin and having my kids grow up with aunts, uncles, and cousins. And Leslie, whose emotional stability was paramount, loved her new high school, had made friends, and was involved in extracurricular activities like theater and women's soccer.

My first step was to set my intention on having another teaching job in the Fall. Each morning before my meditation, I affirmed that the teaching job that I was seeking was seeking me. Then I began looking for a job in every school district within a 30-mile-radius. And last, but by no means least, I lived each day in an attitude of gratitude for the job that was already on its way. And, even though every time I called him, the principal assured me that there were no other jobs available for me, I continued to expect one.

The summer months rolled into the Fall, and I still didn't have a teaching job. Meanwhile, my sister Becky, who was concerned about the kids and me, found a high-paying job for me in the business world. And Leslie, who had adjusted to living in California, kept begging me to take it.

Instead of taking a job I really didn't want, I clung to the words of Dr. Wayne Dyer in his book, The Invisible Force, 365 Ways to Apply the Power of Intention to Your Life. *"Rather than using language indicating that your desires may not materialize, speak from an inner knowing that communicates your profound and simple conviction that your universal Source supplies everything."*

Regardless of how scary things seemed at times, I continued to expect my universal Source to support my intention. And I made sure that my words and actions came from a conviction that the universal Source would supply me with exactly what I needed. *"Trust me, Becky,"* I would say to her, *"we will all be okay! I promise you that I will get a teaching job."*

Since I prefered a substitute teaching job to working in the business world, I called my former principal once again, and inquired about the possibility of substitute teaching.

The tone of his voice led me to believe that he was happy to hear from me. *"Hi, Julie,"* he said enthusiastically. *"I've been thinking about you. I would love to offer you a teaching position. But since you are so low on the totem pole, the only way I can re-hire you is, if you have something to offer that no other tenured teacher in the district has."*

Then he said something that made the hair on the back of my neck stand up on end. *"A year ago,"* he said, *"during your third interview, you mentioned that you had studied French in graduate school. Do you think that you can teach French 1?"*

I couldn't believe my ears! I must admit that for a moment, I began to play small. *"Oh no!"* I thought, *"it has been over ten years since that French class. I can't possibly do that."* Then, after what seemed like a long pause, I decided to play BIG. *"Yes, of course, I can teach French 1"* I replied.

*"Okay then!"* he said. *"Let me get back to you."*

Another premeditated gift that I was free to accept or reject, was waiting in the wings. After scanning one of the largest school districts in California, I was the only teacher available who was credentialed to teach advanced Spanish, French 1, and American literature.

That September, a week after school had officially started, I got the position. And that miracle job, enabled me to begin the process that would eventually take us to the big, beautiful house that I had promised Leslie.

First, I applied for a loan and purchased my first home as a single woman. A year later, when my three-bedroom condo had doubled in value, I purchased another one. Shortly after that, my mother died and left me a small house across town.

Although I was now the proud owner of two, 3-bedroom condos and a small house, none of those properties were as large as the house we had left in Coventry, Connecticut. So, focused on keeping the promise that I had made to Leslie a few years earlier, I set my intention on finding that house. As I pictured it in my mind, the house had four bedrooms with a large living room in which I could meditate, and a large family room for the kids and their friends. It was in a safe neighborhood and of course, it had to be affordable on my teacher's salary.

To attract that house into our lives, I lived each day in an attitude of gratitude for what we already had, and I became willing to forgive those whom I perceived had hurt me.

Each morning after my meditation, I read the following passage from A Course in Miracles. *"Do you want care and safety, and a warmth of sure protection always? Do you want a quietness that cannot be disturbed, a gentleness that never can be hurt, a deep, abiding comfort, and a rest so perfect it can never be upset? All this forgiveness offers you."*

I had once experienced all of that, and more than anything else, I wanted to feel that *'deep, abiding comfort'* again. And I especially wanted to feel it the next time I ran into my ex-husband and his significant other.

I had been working on my forgiveness project for a while when I got a call from Loren who wanted to see the children. Feeling the *'deep, abiding comfort'* that forgiveness offers, I invited him to our condo, and we chatted for a while like friends.

During our conversation, he mentioned that he had become a real estate agent and had a client who wanted to down-size. *"Do you still have the house across town that your mother left you?"* he asked. *"My client, who has a large house in one of the best neighborhoods in town, might be interested in exchanging it for that small house."*

After some negotiations, my promise to Leslie finally came true. We moved into a large, four-bedroom house with a large living and family room, in one of the best neighborhoods in Bakersfield at the time.

*"We can accept things as they really are, or we can relax and embrace the open-endedness of the human situation."*

~Pema Chodron~

# CHAPTER 12

Leslie was sixteen, Rusty, who by then, had changed his name to Russ, was fourteen, and Tom was twelve when they were reunited with their birth dad, whom they had not seen or heard from in over ten years. Seeing his kids again was an emotional experience for Russell Petrone Sr. who sensing their lack of connection to him, set his intention on winning them back.

Since Leslie offered the most resistance, he worked most diligently on her. He took her and her brothers to concerts, nice restaurants, and got her a car of her own. Although It took a few years, Leslie, who was adamant about never changing her name again, finally agreed to adoption and a name change back to Petrone.

After the adoption, their birth dad took his rightful place in their lives. He attended all family gatherings such as Thanksgiving and Christmas celebrations, weddings and christenings. And was also present at high school and college graduations. Two of those memorable events were Leslie's graduation from high school and college—occasions of great joy for all of us, for so many reasons.

Another major change, stemming from the tremendous spiritual growth I had experienced over those years, was that I resigned from teaching and enrolled in seminary.

Leslie, the first to leave home and go away to college, got her degree in marketing and journalism at Chico State the same summer that I was ordained as a Unity minister.

I had been in seminary less than a year when I received a call from Chico State. Leslie, who was twenty-one at the time, had gone to the infirmary with a bad cold and her doctor ordered a sweat test and discovered that Leslie had cystic fibrosis.

The doctor who attended her was so amazed at how healthy she looked, and how strong she was despite having had the disease since birth, that she had the tests run twice. Once the evidence was conclusive, the doctor called me and asked if Leslie knew about her disease.

I explained that Leslie had been diagnosed when she was almost five years old, and, because she had had a spontaneous remission just before she turned eight, I had decided not to mention the disease to her.

The doctor's reaction to my answer was swift. *"People with genetic diseases like cystic fibrosis,"* she said, *"don't have spontaneous remissions."*

I agreed and assured her that according to all I had read about the disease, she was right. *"Yet,"* I continued, *"Leslie did have a spontaneous remission that lasted almost ten years."*

Then I went on to explain why I believed that to be true. I told her how unbelievably well and strong Leslie had been for all those years. I told her that at age eleven, while living in Spain, Leslie had passed her school physical with flying colors and had never even had a cold that year. *"Then,"* I added, *"at fifteen in Connecticut, she joined her high school track team, and ran the 1- mile as well as the 440 relays. Besides that,"* I continued, *"Leslie joined the cross-country team and became one of their best runners. And there had been some buzz about a college scholarship for her."*

The doctor listened to me intently, with no interruptions. Then, with an incredulous look on her face, she smiled warmly and admitted that, although Leslie had had no medication or lung treatments for sixteen years, she looked so healthy and strong that the test had been done twice. And like the doctor at Children's Hospital sixteen years earlier, she also mentioned that the only sign of the disease in Leslie's body was *"the clubbing."*

However, she was quick to remind me that since Leslie was now twenty-one years old, she had to be told about her disease. So, she asked me to fly out to Chico, California and be present when Leslie was told about her condition for the first time.

I arrived at the infirmary in Chico State the next day, and the doctor and I decided that we should walk into Leslie's room together. Leslie was so shocked to see me walk into that infirmary with her doctor, that before I could even say my usual

"Hi, Leslie honey," she screamed, "MOM, WHAT ARE YOU DOING HERE?"

Finding herself in a rather awkward situation, the doctor said, "Leslie, I have asked your mother to be here because we have tested you twice to be sure, and we have found that you have cystic fibrosis."

With a perplexed look on her face, Leslie asked, *"What is cystic fibrosis?"*

*"Cystic fibrosis,"* replied the doctor, *"is a genetic disease that you were born with."* Then she asked Leslie, *"Do you know anything about this disease?*

*"I remember being sick as a child. But my mom told me I had a lung problem and that I had gotten over it"* replied Leslie.

With a deep sense of compassion in her voice, the doctor said, *"Leslie,* we *are going to give you lots of information to take home with you so that you will understand your disease."*

Then she placed her hand on Leslie's shoulder, looked straight into her eyes, and said, *"Leslie, you obviously are an extraordinary woman. If you were able to put a gene-based disease like cystic fibrosis into spontaneous remission once, you should be able to live a fairly normal life of one remission after another."*

At the time, being an extraordinary woman didn't matter to Leslie. All she heard that day was that she had a serious condition that could interfere with her college life and social schedule. Up to that point, Leslie had lived no differently than any of her college friends and wanted to continue doing so.

Thankfully, for the most part, Leslie was able to continue to enjoy her college life and beyond, with very few setbacks.

*"Faith is the bird that feels the light
when the dawn is still dark."*

*~ Rabindranath Tagore~*

# CHAPTER 13

It was Palm Sunday in Tallmadge, Ohio where I served as senior minister of a large Unity church. Spring was in the air and as the greeters at the door passed out palms, the anticipation of Easter Sunday, which was just a week away, was palpable.

Feeling exhausted when I finally got home that Sunday afternoon, I decided to take a nap. I had just fallen asleep when the phone rang. It was Leslie, calling from the hospital in La Jolla, California where she had gone for her bi-yearly tune-up.

"*Mom,*" she said in a very weak, trembling voice, "*please pray for me, I'm very sick. My temperature keeps going up and they can't get it down.*"

"*How high is your temperature?*" I asked.

"*Last night it was 101, and now it is 103,*" she responded.

Feeling extremely concerned, I assured her that I would get my Unity prayer team on it right away, and as a Reiki Master, I would begin sending long distance, healing energy immediately. Then, in the most optimistic voice that I could muster, I told her to hang in there and I would fly to California to be with her after Easter.

However, when I hung up the phone, I felt very troubled, and very anxious to be with Leslie right away. *"How was I to do that?"* I asked myself. Holy Week was a very busy week for large churches. We were expecting over five hundred people to attend our two Easter services, and I still had much to prepare. So, I called Leslie again and told her that since there is no time or space in Spirit, I would be there with her in Spirit.

Feeling very disappointed, Leslie argued that my being there in person would be much more helpful. Then, much too tired to continue talking, she asked if she could hang up.

About half an hour later she called again. *"Mom,"* she whispered, *"I've been sick before, but this time, I don't think I'm going to make it."*

Now she really got my attention. *"Why not, Leslie honey?"* I asked.

*"Because I have never been this sick,"* she said. *"My temperature keeps rising and they can't get it to come down."*

I tried with every reserve of love in my soul to convince her and myself that she would be okay. But as I hung up that phone, I felt an urgency to get to California that I could not explain away. So, I called my board president and explained the situation. She listened with an open heart and agreed that I should go, but not before promising to handle all the Easter preparations while I was gone. An hour later, she called again to tell me that, not only had she made my plane reservation, but her husband had paid for the ticket.

I flew out of Ohio that day and arrived at Thornton Hospital in La Jolla, California late that night. As I walked into Leslie's room and stood by her bed, I realized that she was really in trouble. She had contracted a virus called CMV which could be fatal to people with AIDS. Although Leslie tested negative for AIDS, the doctors could not figure out why she had that full-blown virus. And to make matters worse, at the time, there was no cure.

By Wednesday, her temperature had reached an all-time high of 105 degrees and all she wanted to do was sleep. Trying desperately to keep her awake, I would talk to her and pray aloud for hours as I pushed her wheelchair up and down the halls of the hospital. Then, in another attempt to bring her temperature down, I would return her to her bed, place ice cubes under her arms and feet, climb into her bed and just hold her.

At one point in this process, while I was facing her in a tight embrace, she had a projectile nosebleed that literally blinded me. Shocked and very upset by what had just happened, I instinctively jumped out of her bed, grabbed a towel, and began cleaning the blood out of my stinging eyes. Once help arrived, feeling scared, frustrated, and anxious because nothing seemed to be working, all I wanted to do was to get out of that room.

Fortunately for Leslie and for me, I had a prayer warrior on my Prayer Team in Ohio called Margaret Garrison. Since at the time, there were no cell phones, I raced down the halls of the hospital, frantically looking for a phone booth so I could call her.

As soon as I heard her voice, I calmed down, stopped crying and explained what was happening with Leslie. Margaret prayed and stayed with me on that phone until my anxiety had lessened and I was at peace.

Once back in her room, I returned to my routine of putting ice under her arms and feet. Then, as

I always did, I climbed into her bed and held her burning body tightly in my arms until morning.

Still lying next to her in her bed, I awoke to a room filled with smiling doctors and nurses talking to each other in hushed tones. When they noticed that I was awake, they reported that Leslie's temperature had gone down during the night from 105 to 101.

I literally jumped out of her bed, and unable to contain my joy and sense of gratitude, I started jumping up and down. All the while, crying *"Thank you, thank you, Thank you God!"* Meanwhile, Leslie, who with a temperature of 101, was still pretty much out of it, slept through it all.

During that week at Thornton Hospital in La Jolla, California, I learned that there is a gift in every seeming tragedy. Leslie and I had suffered a crucifixion and experienced a glorious resurrection during Holy Week.

My precious girl, who at age thirty-one was almost dead, had risen to a new life full of possibilities, including a beautiful wedding and another nineteen years of life. Happy and infinitely grateful, I boarded my flight to Ohio for the most uplifting and profound Easter Sunday of my life.

*"Think not that you can direct the course of love, for love, if it finds you worthy, directs your course."*

~ Kahlil Gibran~

# CHAPTER 14

Leslie continued to triumph over cystic fibrosis, milestone after milestone and year after year. After her college graduation, she continued to follow her dreams, embarking on both a happy marriage and a satisfying career.

Meaningful relationships were of such primary importance to Leslie, that after graduation, she and her friends from Chico State created a tradition that kept their friendships strong throughout her lifetime. Every Summer, during the month of August, she and a group of her friends rented a houseboat and spent a week on a large lake enjoying a fun-filled class reunion.

During one of those joyously anticipated Chico State class reunions, Leslie met Bill Hopkins, who was there as the guest of one of Leslie's friends. Meeting Bill, whom everyone called Morti, turned out to be perfect timing for Leslie who was still smarting over the loss of a two-year, college, love affair. It was love at first sight for Morti and "Petrone," as he always called her. And they became inseparable.

When Morti learned that Leslie had cystic fibrosis, he realized that he had come to a crossroads in his life. Morti, who had always wanted to have a long, happy marriage and a family of his own, now faced a major choice. He could spend his life with a beautiful, amazing woman who came with the risk of a potentially shortened lifespan, and with whom he might not be able to have a family, or he could play it safe. He could wait for someone who could provide him with the potential of a long and happy, married life and a family.

Morti chose life with that beautiful, amazing woman: Leslie. Shortly after making that life-altering decision, a friend asked him if he had considered all the ramifications of marrying a woman with a chronic disease like cystic fibrosis.

Morti's reply was swift. *"It is too late to worry about that!"* he said. *"I've already fallen in love with her."* And years later, when I asked him what having to take care of Leslie had been like for him, He said, *"I didn't have to take care of Leslie. Leslie always took care of me!"*

Over nineteen years later, when Leslie was celebrating her fiftieth birthday in a hospital intensive care unit, Morti told me that his decision to spend those years with Leslie had really been an easy one. And he followed up that comment by saying, *"If given the opportunity, I would do it again in a heartbeat."*

I was serving as a Unity minister in an English-speaking ministry in San Juan, Puerto Rico when I got a call from Leslie telling me that she and Morti were engaged and planning to get married. And to sweeten the pot, she asked me to officiate at their wedding.

Leslie, who was thirty-five at the time, had a fairytale wedding. She rode to the chapel in a beautifully decorated chariot pulled by four white horses. Everyone stood up as she entered through the large, opened doors of the chapel. Like a breath of fresh air, she gracefully moved down that long aisle with her birth father, Russell Petrone Sr., at her right side, and her stepfather, Loren Johnson, whom she still called "*daddy*," on her left.

When they reached the altar, Leslie kissed her two fathers, and handed her beautiful bouquet of white flowers to her maid of honor. Then, with an energy of love and connection that was palpable, she and Morti stood before me and exchanged their sacred vows of matrimony.

A few days later, the happy couple left for Italy where they had an unforgettable honeymoon. During that week in Italy, they never missed anything on their agenda. When too much walking or hill climbing caused Leslie to gasp for breath, Morti would simply pick her up and carry her on his shoulders.

Just as he had done in Italy, during their fifteen-year marriage, Morti continued to carry Leslie up the hills and down the valleys of her illness. During those times when her condition frightened her, she simply cried out *"**Morti!**"* And always, his immediate response was to hold her tightly in his arms and say, *"It's okay, baby, I gotcha!"*

*"Focus all of your energy
not on fighting the old, but
on building the new."*

*~Socrates~*

# CHAPTER 15

As a very successful, sales manager at the Russ Berry Corporation, a large giftware company, Leslie had earned a buying trip to China with her employer.

Since at the time, smoking was permitted on airplane flights, Leslie had a very, difficult time breathing or trying to fall asleep in that smoke-filled cabin. Consequently, when she finally arrived in China, she was exhausted. To make things even worse, she spent a week in smoke-filled rooms, buying merchandise with an employer who chain-smoked cigars.

Getting very little rest and inhaling all that smoke made Leslie very weak and lethargic. Her boss, who didn't know about her disease, expressed disappointment that she wasn't acting like the enthusiastic, bubbly woman whose high sales record had earned her this buying trip to China.

Unfortunately, that trip to China that she had been so proud of winning, turned out to be her undoing. She was so sick that she had to be hospitalized.

Ever since that day in the Infirmary of Chico state when she had been told about her disease, Leslie had insisted on keeping her condition a secret. Because at that time, many people suffered from "smokers cough," few if any, ever questioned her about her coughing. And if anyone did, Leslie told them she was simply getting over a cold. And when she returned home from China and had to be hospitalized, she told her employer, colleagues and friends, that she was suffering from a bad case of exhaustion.

However, her "coming out" happened a year later, at a leadership conference in a luxurious hotel in Santa Fe, New Mexico. Leslie, who at thirty-eight was one of the most successful sales managers in her company, was to be promoted to vice president of sales at this conference.

The moment she arrived in Santa Fe, Leslie noticed that she was having difficulty catching her breath. As she walked out of the elevator and down the hall, on her way to the conference room where the promotion ceremony was to be held, she began to feel very lightheaded. Trying desperately to catch her breath, she walked very slowly before stopping and leaning against the wall.

Unfortunately, at the time, she didn't realize that it was the high altitude in Santa Fe that was creating her breathing problems. So panic-stricken at not being able to breathe for the first time in her life, she fainted and had to be revived with oxygen.

After that frightening incident, Leslie decided to stop trying to hide the fact that she had a serious lung problem and told her employer and colleagues that she had cystic fibrosis. The sense of relief that her "coming out" created for her was incredible. Now she could go to the hospital openly, get her treatments, and have her family and friends visit.

Before Santa Fe, Leslie had been incredibly strong and enthusiastic. She returned to California feeling weak and was frequently short of breath. Thinking that she was dying had created so much psychological damage for her that she spoke more slowly, was less confident; and even her appearance began to change. Worst of all, her weakened state had convinced most of us as well, that her life would soon be over.

Shortly after the Santa Fe incident, her employer's wife, who was very concerned about Leslie's condition, suggested that Leslie go to see Andrew

Weil, MD, a pioneer in the new field of integrative medicine whose practice was in Tucson, Arizona.

Still afraid of flying, Leslie declined. And her employer's wife begged her to reconsider. *"Leslie,"* she pleaded, *"if anyone can help you, I know he can.*

*Besides,"* she added, *"it usually takes eighteen months to get an appointment with Dr. Weil—and you already have one."*

With great trepidation about flying so soon after the incident in Santa Fe, Leslie finally agreed to make the trip. But feeling too weak to make that trip alone, she asked me to go with her. Her employer's wife was so happy with Leslie's decision that she gifted us with a "mother/daughter" week at the world-famous Canyon Ranch in Tucson.

Walking slowly while holding on to my arm, Leslie and I boarded a plane for Tucson. As we sat down, I exchanged greetings with the woman sitting next to me in the window seat who seemed very friendly—until Leslie started coughing. The frightened woman immediately reached into her purse for a tissue, covered her face, buried her head in the window and called for a flight attendant.

Trying to make the frightened woman feel better, I explained, *"My daughter's cough is not contagious." She has a lung disease called cystic fibrosis."* Digging her face deeper into the window, the fear-based woman would have no part of my explanation. Soon, a flight attendant arrived, and the woman insisted on being moved to another seat which was very upsetting for Leslie.

That experience unnerved Leslie so much that she told me that, after her consultation with Dr. Weil, she just wanted to go back home to San Diego. *"Does that mean that you want to pass on the Mother/Daughter week at the Canyon Ranch in Tucson?"* I asked.

*"I'm sorry Mom,"* she answered, *"but I feel much too weak for anything like that."* Unable to hide my disappointment with her decision, we pushed our way through the busy Tucson airport, rented a car, and drove the twenty miles to Dr. Andrew Weil's office in total silence.

Dr. Weil's warm smile and peace-filled demeanor put us both immediately at ease. Leslie, who was still very upset over the incident on the airplane, and had been feeling too weak to stand up straight since the Santa Fe incident, stood with her head slightly bent as if she were examining the beautiful Spanish tiles on the floor.

"*Hello, Leslie,*" Dr. Weil said enthusiastically. "*Welcome to Tucson!*" Seeing how depressed and weak Leslie seemed, before asking her any questions, he invited her to sit down in front of him.

Having reviewed her medical history before her arrival, he mentioned none of it. Instead, he said, "*Leslie, tell me all about your life.*" In a very, weak voice, with her head slightly bent, Leslie told him about her spontaneous remission, her high school and college life, her meaningful marriage to Morti, her loving family, her successful work life, and the Santa Fe incident that had finally led her to him.

Dr. Weil listened intently without a single interruption. Then, he did something that surprised both of us. He asked Leslie to stop talking and just be silent for a little while. After sitting in total silence for a few minutes, the doctor asked Leslie to stand in front of him so that he could observe her.

Leslie stood up slowly, walked toward him, and stood before him in total silence. After a few minutes, Doctor Weil broke the silence by saying, "*Leslie, I see years of life in front of you!*" He let that proclamation sink in, before following up with, *"and I am going to give you a regimen of vitamins and minerals that will really help you."*

Hearing such assurance from a renowned physician who had not only written a book on the New York Times Best seller list, but was acclaimed as *"America's Health Guru,"* did more for Leslie than the new regimen of vitamins and minerals he prescribed.

In fact, I think that,*"**Leslie, I see years of life in front of you!**"* was all she really heard that day. Those words had such a beneficent, psychological effect on Leslie that she walked out of his office with her head held high as if she were preparing to live again.

Leslie was feeling so very much alive again, that before returning to San Diego, we drove directly to the Canyon Ranch in Tucson, and enjoyed an unforgettable mother/daughter week.

A month after we had returned from Tucson, Leslie was having dinner with her husband at a restaurant in San Diego when a man nearby heard her cough and asked her if she had a cold. Remembering the frightened woman on our flight to Tucson earlier, she said, a bit sarcastically, *"No, I don't have a cold!*

*But, don't worry, you can't catch what I have! I have cystic fibrosis."*

The man, who happened to be a drug rep for a large pharmaceutical company, enthusiastically said, *"I thought so!"* Next, he suggested that she try a specific inhaler sold by his company for people with lung problems.

That inhaler, combined with her other medications and the regimen of vitamins and minerals from Dr. Andrew Weil not only made her very strong again, but had her affirming for the next ten years, **"I may have cystic fibrosis, but cystic fibrosis does not have me."**

*"Life is not measured by the number of breaths we take, but by the moments that take our breath away."*

*~ Anonymous ~*

# CHAPTER 16

No matter how she was health-wise, Leslie never forgot a birthday, anniversary, or any occasion that was meaningful to others. She hosted Thanksgiving for our family and decorated our Christmas trees. And she always called her younger brothers to make sure they joined her at my Easter and Christmas services.

Wise beyond her years, Leslie was always the go-to person for her brothers and me whenever we needed sound advice or just a listening ear. And like her grandpa Victor, she became the glue that held our family together.

In her thirties, Leslie only went once a year for her ten-day checkups and lived pretty well for the rest of the year. In her early forties, she began going twice a year. Then, as she reached her late forties, the hospital visits increased exponentially.

Despite the fact that her ten-day hospital stays consisted of intravenous antibiotic medication, lung vest treatments, postural drainage, pulmonary function tests, and gastrointestinal medications,

Leslie never let the routine get in the way of quality time with those she loved.

This was equally true when she was at home. I clearly remember one Saturday morning when Leslie was in her forties. She was lying on her king-sized bed receiving a lung treatment from Morti. Propped up on her pillows, I was sitting next to her watching TV, while her brother Tom, at the foot of the bed, was working on his laptop.

That day, as I took in the visual of all of us comfortably doing our own thing on Leslie's bed while she was getting a treatment, I realized how perfectly my original intention of making Leslie's life as normal as possible was playing out.

During the years that I lived in Orange County and then in San Diego, Leslie and I had created an adventure out of her *"ten-day tune-ups"* as the family called them. Knowing that, as a minister, Saturdays and Sundays were busy days for me, Leslie always set those two days apart for quality time with Morti. And Mondays and Tuesdays, my days off, were reserved for me.

Sleeping on a cot in her room or in her bed, there were times when I was awakened in the middle of the night because she was afraid and just needed me to hold her hand, comfort her, pray with her. But most of the time, we watched movies in bed and took walks around the grounds or in the halls, depending on how strong she felt at the time.

In between treatments, we ate meals together, talked with hospital staff, laughed a lot, and shared our deepest secrets. Although I was devoted to her as a mother, we also shared a powerful sense of sisterhood that transcended the mother-daughter relationship.

I think one of the greatest things I ever did for Leslie was to model for her the importance of sisterhood. Leslie's friendships with women lasted throughout her entire lifetime. In fact, she took her last breath in the presence of her husband and her friend Luann. And at her memorial service, fifteen women claimed her as their closest friend.

In fact, sisterhood was so important to us that we shared one of the most meaningful experiences of our lives at a ten-day women's retreat. Leslie was 44 by then, and with her portable oxygen tank on her back, without a single complaint, she did everything the rest of us were called to do.

During the closing ceremony of that amazing retreat, forming a large circle, we all spontaneously reached out to take each other's hand. As we stood there, ninety women strong, sharing the powerful energy of feminine oneness and sisterhood, I spotted Leslie on the opposite side of the circle just as she spotted me.

Standing across from each other in an energetic embrace, not just as mother and daughter but as two grown women with a lifelong friendship, we received an unexpected bonus.

In that holy instant, with our eyes locked on each other and our hearts beating as one, we both heard a very, familiar song begin to ring across the sky. As the words of the song, *"I Am Woman,"* by Helen Reddy, which had been a catalyst to both of us in finding our strength and courage as women, began to fill the space where we were standing, we became unaware of anyone else in that circle but the two of us.

Smiling and listening to the words of that familiar song with open and receptive hearts, it seemed like we were both remembering and confirming the marvelous, 44-year journey we had just taken together.

*"I once asked a bird, 'How is it that you fly in this gravity of darkness?' She responded, 'Love lifts me'."*

~ Hafiz~

# CHAPTER 17

In October of 2005, I went to Peru, as part of a group that consisted of ten spiritual leaders from various religions, twelve people from all walks of life, plus a shaman waiting for us there. This experience turned out to be life-transforming, not only for me but, two years later, for Leslie as well.

After a week in Peru, about half of our group had developed intestinal issues and such severe mosquito bites that a few had to be hospitalized. Consequently, when the day arrived for our dawn climb to Machu Picchu, only ten people showed up. And of the ten that started the climb early that foggy morning, only the shaman, my friend, and I were fortunate enough to reach the peak.

As the three of us were nearing the top of the mountain, the shaman pointed out a beautiful falcon perched on a rock, looking in our direction. And he told us that, since the falcon is a messenger of the condor, its presence was a good omen.

After an exhilarating climb, we finally arrived at the top of the mountain. Exhausted and light-headed due to the high altitude, my friend and I were sitting on a flat rock trying to catch our breath when the shaman approached us.

He welcomed us to the mountain top, shook our hands, and congratulated us for having been the only ones to make it to the peak. Then, explaining that the number three was a very mystical number, he told us that something that he had experienced only once before, when he had been at the peak with his two masters, was going to occur again. He was going to summon a condor from the sky.

As we listened with bated breath, he reminded us of the falcon we had seen on our way up the mountain. Then he said that, as its messenger, the falcon had already alerted the condor that it was going to be summoned. Although we had learned that the condor was considered the mystical messenger of the people of Peru, that was the extent of our knowledge of Peruvian mysticism. However, when the shaman excitedly told us to fix our gaze into that empty sky, we knew that something extremely mystical was about to happen.

Climbing on a flat rock, the shaman began frantically waving his arms toward a sky that seemed devoid of anything but clouds. Moving back and forth quickly, he began to call out some mystical incantations in a native language that neither of us understood. I must admit that, at first, the shaman's quick movements not only seemed strange to me, but I worried that he might slip and fall to the valley below. However, committed to becoming a part of his mystical experience, I released all judgment and just locked my eyes on him.

Fifteen thousand feet above the valley floor, looking into the empty sky with the shaman, I suddenly experienced what A Course in Miracles calls a "*Holy Instant.*" I not only felt totally "at one" with the Shaman and his rituals, but with my friend, the blue sky above me, the mountain, and the valley below.

Basking in the warm glow of that wonderful feeling, I began to realize that the empowering energy of the entire scene had not only lifted me to a place of oneness, but the serene look on my friend's face suggested that she was having a similar reaction. In that blissful state, as if on cue, we both pointed our cameras to the empty sky and waited for the mystical moment.

Even though I was wearing sunglasses, after ten minutes of staring with a frozen gaze toward the morning sky, my eyes, which have always been sensitive to light, began to burn so badly that I was forced to look away.

I removed my sunglasses and began searching frantically in my backpack for eye drops. I had just dropped some medicine in my eyes when my friend excitedly screamed, *"JULIE! PUT YOUR SUNGLASSES BACK ON! THERE IS A BIRD COMING OUT OF THE CLOUDS...IT COULD BE A CONDOR!"*

At that point, the bird flying in the distant sky was much too far away for recognition. However, the shaman, who knew without a doubt that it was a condor, began jumping up and down while waving his arms up to the sky and saying something we simply could not understand. *"I think he is thanking the condor for showing up,"* said my friend.

I adjusted my sunglasses and gazed up at the sky again. Much to my surprise, the bird not only got closer, but began circling around our heads. *"Oh, my God,"* we both gasped as we took one picture after another, *"it IS a condor!"*

Overcome with emotion, tears rolled down the shaman's face as he waited for us to take pictures of the condor. Then, as if he could wait no longer, he put his arms around our shoulders and assured us that the mystical experience that we had just witnessed would not have been possible had there been more than three of us on the mountain top that morning. Then he added, *"it would not have happened if it had been anyone but the three of us."*

With his arms still on our shoulders, he promised us that as participants of that rare, mystical event, we would each experience a miracle of our own when we returned to the United States. Caught up in that powerful promise, I joyously began my descent down that steep, Peruvian mountain.

Three days after my mountaintop experience with the shaman, still, in a blissful space, I boarded the plane for California. All through that October night, on the long flight from Peru to California, my mind was spinning with the prospect of a miracle for Leslie. If not a cure for cystic fibrosis I thought, perhaps there would be another spontaneous remission.

The last two months of 2005 quietly morphed into 2006. Although Leslie, who was forty-five at the time, was still quite strong and well, there had been no cure for CF that year and nothing miraculous had taken place.

Thinking that perhaps I had missed the miraculous in 2006 by not being fully present, I decided to bring in 2007 in a very spiritual, meaningful space. So, I headed to northern California to a yoga retreat, and ushered in the year in a peace-filled, expectant state of mind.

Although there was no spontaneous remission or a cure for cystic fibrosis in the year 2007, there was a premeditated gift waiting in the wings for Leslie and me that we could either accept or reject.

*"Synchronicity is an ever present reality."*

Carl Jung

# CHAPTER 18

As the senior minister of the Unity Community Church of Brea, California, the first thing I did when I arrived at church each Sunday morning was to turn off my cell phone and place it on the lectern before moving to center stage. The PowerPoint message on the screen, as well as my silenced phone in clear view, reminded congregants to do likewise.

Leslie and her brothers never called me on Sunday mornings, knowing I was leading the service at my church. However, an accident of chance caused me to forget to turn off my phone that morning. I simply placed it on the lectern and moved to the center.

It was the last Sunday in February of 2007. Although the Sunday service was generally only packed on special Sundays like Easter and Christmas, for some inexplicable reason, the church was full that day. The musicians, who had been exceptionally good that morning, were receiving a standing ovation, and I was waiting for the applause to die down so that we could end the service by singing The Peace Song.

Although I don't have an exceptional singing voice, music has always been meaningful to me and the music on my ringtone attested to that. Sometimes, I would get so caught up listening to the music that I would forget to answer the phone.

A case in point: that Sunday, the congregation was already standing, poised to sing The Peace Song when music, coming from the top of my lectern, began to fill the room.

At first, it seemed surreal to hear some of my favorite music in the sanctuary.

Of course, I knew it could not be my phone, because I was sure that I had silenced it, as always. So, with a smile on my face, I just stood there at center stage trying to figure out who in the congregation was the culprit. Then, as if awakening from a bad dream, I realized where the sound was coming from. *"Oh, my God," I thought, "it's MY phone that's ringing!"*

Deeply chagrined, I just stood there staring at the lectern. Suddenly, a congregant began to laugh aloud, and soon another joined in, then I did too. Now the entire room was filled with raucous laughter. Not only had the sound of my cell phone changed the energy in the room, but because of my insistence that we all silence our phones every Sunday, the joke was on me.

Convinced that it had to be a wrong number, I walked across the stage to turn off the phone and resume closing the service. But as I reached for the phone, I noticed the name of the caller. It was Leslie!

Unable to breathe and on her way to ICU, Leslie had interrupted my service with a call for help. Gasping for breath, she whispered, *"Mom," I …Can't… breathe. They…are… taking me …to ICU. I need you! PLEASE….HURRY!"*

Leslie, who was 45 at the time, had been going to Thornton Hospital in La Jolla, California for her tune-up for the past 15 years. And none of us had ever worried about it. However, the absolute terror that I heard in her voice warned me that this time, the situation would be quite different.

As I grabbed my purse and began pushing my way through the standing congregation, I heard a woman say to the person standing next to her, *"Where is Reverend Julie going in such a hurry? We haven't sung the Peace Song or had our closing prayer yet."*

The shock on my face said it all. Without a word to anyone except the prayer chaplain, I moved quickly to the back of the room. As I reached the door, I shouted, *"Kathy, please call Silent Unity! Tell them to pray for my daughter Leslie, who is in real trouble."* (Silent Unity is Unity's worldwide prayer ministry.)

Then, I rushed out the door, ran across the busy street, got into my car, and drove the longest eighty-five miles of my life.

*"Courage is fear that has said its prayers."*

~ Anne Lamott~

# CHAPTER 19

Growing up in New York City, where subways and buses were always available and there was never anywhere to park a car, driving had never become natural to me.

I rode a subway to school from sixth grade through high school. Soon after that, I got married and my husband did all the driving. So, unlike Leslie, who had been driving since she was sixteen, I got my driver's license in my late twenties and seldom, if ever, had to use it.

Most of my career as a minister had been in states other than California, so I never had had to drive on a freeway. When I arrived in California as the minister of Unity of Brea in Orange County, I thought I could get away with driving only on side streets. However, it didn't take long to realize that if I wanted to go anywhere, I would have to learn to drive on those scary, California freeways.

With much trepidation, I would venture onto a freeway, miss my exit, go twenty miles out of my way, find myself hopelessly lost, and call Leslie, who had become my personal, GPS system. After months of missing my exit and having to get bailed out by Leslie, I decided to learn how to navigate my way through the California freeway system.

Since driving bumper to bumper at 80 miles an hour was not in my comfort zone, I usually stayed in the right lane where I could drive the exact speed limit and never have to pass a car, or—God forbid—a truck.

Although I've always been assertive in my personal life and career, each time I got behind the wheel, my lack of confidence in driving became very evident. *"Be more aggressive, Mom,"* Leslie would say during those rare times when she was sitting in the passenger seat. Leslie, who always grabbed the keys when we went anywhere together in my car, used to joke about my driving. *"My mom,"* she would say to her friends, *"will drive behind a truck for 500 miles rather than pass it."* I must admit that there was much truth to that statement.

I certainly had never prepared myself for the driving experience that awaited me on that last Sunday of February in 2007. Wearing three-inch heels, and Ignoring my trick ankle, I ran across a very busy street to my parked car. I got behind the wheel, strapped myself in, and headed for the freeway.

My focus that day was on one thing only: getting to that hospital in time to answer Leslie's call for help. As I always did, I began a prayer of gratitude before the fact. *"Thank you, God, for getting me to the hospital safely and with plenty of time to help Leslie. Amen."*

Still feeling somewhat anxious, I began to affirm one of my favorite passages from A Course in Miracles: *"The peace of God is all I want, the peace of God is my one goal, it is the aim of all my living here, the end I seek..."* Knowing that the subconscious mind requires repetition; in a trembling voice, I affirmed that statement again and again.

Soon, the anxiety began to dissipate, and I began to feel centered, alert, and focused. In that state of mind, I remembered that when I was a minister in Ohio, and Leslie and her brothers Russell, Tom, and Eric lived in California, I would affirm Unity's Prayer of Protection. Holding their picture in front of me, I would say, *"Leslie, Russell, Tom and Eric, the Light of God surrounds us, the love of God enfolds us, the power of God protects us, the presence of God watches over us. Wherever we are, God is, and all is well."* Despite the distance between us, that prayer always filled me with an incredible sense of connection and oneness with all four of my children.

Wanting desperately to feel that same spiritual connection to Leslie at that moment, I began to affirm, *"Leslie honey, the light of God surrounds us, the love of God enfolds us, the Power of God protects us, the presence of God watches over us. Wherever we are, God is, and all is well."* As I drove those eighty miles, I kept picturing Leslie's beautiful face while affirming the prayer.

Soon, all fear and apprehension about driving left me. And doing what had previously seemed impossible, I found myself speeding down the left lane, bumper to bumper, at 85 miles an hour. Fearlessly passing every car and truck in my way, I shouted, *"LESLIE, YOU SHOULD SEE ME NOW!"*

Not only did I arrive safely with time to spare while Leslie was still conscious, but, on that infamous Sunday, I became a seasoned, California, freeway driver.

*"Around the corner, there may wait a new road or a secret gate."*

~J.R.R. Tolkien~

# CHAPTER 20

Leslie, who wanted me to live closer to her in San Diego, had spent lots of time helping me to find a perfect apartment only five miles from her house. However, after giving the long, daily commute to Orange County more thought, I decided against it, and Leslie and I had argued about it. Although we had made up, things between us were still a bit tense. So, I was desperate to reach her while she was still conscious, to make sure things were right between us.

Throughout her entire 45-year struggle with cystic fibrosis, Leslie had never been in ICU. So, it was difficult for me to understand how Leslie could be happily watching movies in her room on Saturday; and gasping for breath in the ICU on Sunday.

However, as I later discovered, Leslie had not maintained her ideal weight and her disease had starved her body of essential nutrients. So, she had checked into the hospital for her bi-yearly checkup in a state of severe malnutrition.

Normally, we breathe in oxygen and exhale carbon dioxide, a waste gas that needs to get out. The way to get it out is by breathing in oxygen. If there is not enough oxygen getting to the brain, the carbon dioxide begins to build, causing among other things, a drop in the body's natural pH-balance. This was what was happening to Leslie.

Leslie's eyes seemed lifeless, and she was extremely disoriented and confused when I entered her room. Trying desperately to get some oxygen to her brain had left her so exhausted that she could barely speak. Despite the BiPAP machine that covered her nose and mouth, enough oxygen still was not getting to Leslie's lungs, so her brain was filling up with carbon dioxide. As I entered her ICU unit at Thornton Hospital and approached her bed, Leslie grabbed my hand in a very tight grip. Although she was unable to speak, the frightened look in her eyes spelled terror. As she looked up at me, her pleading eyes seemed to say, *"DEAR GOD! What is happening to me? I CAN'T BREATHE! What is going on? PLEASE, PLEASE, MOM, HELP ME!"*

Remembering that miracles are expressions of love and anything that comes from love is a miracle, I realized that there could be no shortage of love in that room. So, Ignoring the intense feelings of fear that I had felt when I entered that ICU room, I smiled and said, *"Hi, Leslie Honey!"*

As I said her name, my guidance was not to focus on why this was happening to her, but to focus on what I could do about it. So, I said a quick, silent prayer asking God to help me remember what my real purpose was. Then, putting all my fears aside, I walked over to Leslie and responded to her call for help.

Fighting back tears, I began coaching her, as I had done so many times before. *"Breathe deeply, honey,"* I told her. *"Come on, I'll breathe with you, let's take a very deep breath, together. "I know you can do it."*

I knew that if I encouraged her to take those deep breaths with me, she would at least give it a try. Silently affirming that the oxygen was reaching her brain, I continued to coach her until she began to breathe normally again.

By now, it was 4:00 PM and I had not had anything to eat or drink since 6:00 AM. My blood sugar had dropped, and I was feeling light-headed. And since the breathing situation seemed to be under control, I asked Leslie if I could go grab a cup of coffee. She smiled and motioned for me to go, and I ran to the cafeteria. Fifteen minutes later, I returned to a room in absolute chaos.

I approached my daughter's bed, took her hands in mine, and prayed. Then I tried to get her to breathe in unison with me as we had done before, but it was obvious that as hard as she tried, it was not going to happen. Leslie could no longer get oxygen to her lungs, and the carbon dioxide was building.

Even though I had lived through other catastrophic events with Leslie and had always been a pillar of strength for her, I had never felt as impotent and helpless as I did at that moment.

Although Leslie had been on oxygen 24/7 since she was 45, this was the first time since her experience in Santa Fe, years earlier, that she simply had not been able to get air to her lungs.

At that point, the doctor walked into the room and said, *"I'm sorry, Leslie, but this just is not working."* He explained that the carbon dioxide was building up so fast that Leslie had to be put on a breathing machine immediately, "Or," he warned, *"it will be too late."*

Knowing that women with cystic fibrosis seldom, if ever, survive a breathing machine, Leslie shook her head violently from side to side, refusing to do it. In fact, as weak as she was, she even managed to get a clear *"No!"* out of her mouth.

*"Leslie, are you saying you don't want to be put on the breathing machine?"* asked the doctor.

*"Yes!"* she gasped. Terrified at the thought of losing her, Morti and I asked her why? *"Because I won't come back,"* she answered.

In a firm yet compassionate voice, the doctor then said to her, *"Okay, Leslie, then say good-bye to your husband and mother. I will sedate you and make you as comfortable as possible until you take your last breath."*

The doctor's directive threw Morti and me into a tailspin of panic that had us begging her to accept the intubation. Choking on his tears, Morti implored her, *"PLEASE, PLEASE DO IT, BABY!"* Then he whispered in her ear, *"Please do it! Do it for me baby!*

From a deep place of knowing that she would be okay if she agreed to be intubated, I promised her that we would be there when she woke up. Finally, with death as her only option, Leslie touched Morti's tear-soaked face and said, *"I love you, Morti!"*

Weeping as he held her in his arms, Morti said, *"I love you too, baby!"*

Then just as she was about to be intubated, she looked up at me and gasped, *"I love you, Mom! Are we okay?"*

In that HOLY INSTANT, when any remaining tension between us had dissolved into a place of unconditional love, I answered, *"We are more than okay, Leslie Honey!"*

Still in Morti's arms, Leslie looked at both of us and smiled the most beautiful smile I had ever seen on her face. Then she signaled the doctor to give her the injection which would put her in an induced coma for five days.

The doctor then asked us to leave the room while they put Leslie on a breathing machine. Exhausted and overwhelmed, Morti and I silently crept toward the door. The stress of trying so hard to be brave in front of Leslie, while fighting back the fear of losing her, had worn us out. Clinging to the hope that she would survive that breathing machine had taken all the courage we could muster to keep from breaking out into uncontrollable sobs.

Although Leslie and I had gone through many traumas together, some more serious than others during her forty-six-year-battle with cystic fibrosis, we had never faced anything like this. As serious as things had seemed at times, I must admit that, the possibility of sudden death, like what had almost happened in that ICU room, had never even occurred to me.

Caught up in a very deep sense of anxiety and sadness, we stumbled like two walking zombies into the crowded, waiting room. We were both crying softly when Leslie's doctor walked into the room, stood directly in front of us and whispered, *"You can go in and see her now."*

Morti and I stood up, and with great trepidation, slowly walked toward the ICU room and stepped inside. As we spontaneously looked across the room to her bed, we were both astonished!

The person whom we saw in that bed was far from the frightened, exhausted, malnourished, bedraggled woman whom we had just left. Much to our happy surprise, the transformation we saw in Leslie could only be described as AMAZING.

Leslie looked wonderful! There was so much color in her previously pale lips that it seemed as if someone had put lipstick on her. The stress lines on her forehead were gone and her sunken cheeks looked full and pink. The terror in those big brown eyes that had caused us such deep, emotional trauma, was hiding under her closed eyelids. Her long, dark hair, spread neatly on her pillow, made her look not only peaceful, but stunning. In short: despite the breathing tube and tape tightly pulled across her mouth, Leslie looked sensational!

Morty and I stood there smiling down at her, and at each other. Then, brimming over with love and gratitude as we observed the unbelievable change in our precious girl, we joined in a warm embrace.

For the first time in her life, at the age of 45, Leslie had been put on a breathing machine. At that point in time, no other adult woman with cystic fibrosis at Thornton Hospital in La Jolla, had ever survived it.

And yet, in that love-filled moment, although neither of us knew how it would happen, without a doubt, Morti and I knew that Leslie would survive this unbelievable nightmare and come back to us.

*"The greatest soul growth can be hidden in life's greatest crisis."*

~Viktor Frankl~

# CHAPTER 21

Knowing that I had powerful prayer support behind me gave me strength as I stood by Leslie's bed, day after day, centered on the idea that her Spirit, not her body, was the altar of Truth.

The day before Leslie's cell phone rang during my church service, sending me off on that frantic ride to the hospital in San Diego, I had been the guest speaker at the Science of Mind Practitioners Forum in Orange County.

That very Saturday morning, as I spoke to the Science of Mind Practitioners Forum, Leslie had checked into Thornton Hospital for her ten-day tune-up. Before leaving for my speaking engagement, I had called Leslie at the hospital and found her happily watching a movie.

In my presentation, I spoke to the attendees about Leslie's journey and my part in it. I certainly never could have dreamed that the very next day, Leslie would be in crisis and the powerful healers who had attended my presentation would be concentrating all their healing energy on her.

Committed to keeping our promise to Leslie when she was intubated, Morti and I set our intention to doing whatever was humanly possible to ensure that Leslie would wake up from her 5-day, induced coma as the woman we remembered.

A Course in Miracles says that "*a miracle is a sudden shift into invisibility away from the bodily level.*" We created an environment for Leslie that we hoped would make it easier for her to make that shift, into the healing Light of love. Once we felt that we had done everything we possibly could to make that happen, we stepped out of the way, and let the God presence in Leslie aided by her fabulous medical team, do the rest.

The intention that Morti and I set into motion required not only a real connection between him and me, but a oneness of purpose and my unwavering faith in God's healing love.

After setting the intention that Leslie would wake up from her coma returning to us as the woman we loved and remembered, our first action step was to decide that only HEALING LOVE would be welcome in Leslie's ICU room.

Since love and fear are mutually exclusive and one cannot exist in the presence of the other, Morti and I agreed that fear had to be a stranger in Leslie's presence.

To ensure that Leslie would be surrounded only by loving, positive, lifting, healing thoughts during this crisis, we decided that only Morti, and I would be allowed in her room. However, because the late Alice Johnson, had been instrumental in helping me to change my thinking about the possibility of a spontaneous remission for Leslie, we also invited her son Loren to join us in this endeavor.

The decision to keep her brothers, birth father, family and close friends out of that ICU room was difficult at best. We knew that they loved her, and that she adored them. But because they loved her so much, we felt that seeing her in a coma could trigger fear issues around losing her.

Morti's job, which was perfect for his sweet, laid back personality, was to explain to family and friends why they would not be allowed entrance in Leslie's room. He also kept them posted on her progress and invited them to support us in seeing her healed and whole.

Since thoughts are the first level of creation, words are the second level, and action is the third, we focused on all three. Constantly reassuring Leslie's subconscious mind that *'mighty currents of God's healing love were moving through every cell of her body,* we placed a headset of positive songs and affirmations on her head every morning.

A Course in Miracles says, *"The memory of God comes to the quiet mind. It cannot come where there is conflict, for a mind at war against itself remembers not eternal gentleness."*

To help create a peace-filled mind that was free of conflict, our daily, 12-hour vigil included silent prayer, meditation and just silently loving her. Whether praying, meditating or reading, we sat or stood by Leslie's bed in an attitude of gratitude for the healing that was taking place in her.

Morti and I arrived each day at 7:00 AM and left at 7:00 PM. To ensure that one of us never left her side, we took turns eating breakfast and lunch. Her stepfather Loren, who arrived at 7:30 PM continued the vigil. In a quiet voice that would not disturb the doctors, nurses, and hospital staff, he read positive, healing passages to Leslie until 10:00 PM when he quietly slipped out of her ICU room.

Additionally, as Leslie's advocates, Morti and I paid careful attention to all her medical procedures and medications and worked harmoniously with her doctors and medical team.

*"Love is the greatest healing force in the world; nothing goes deeper than Love. It heals not only the Body, not only the Mind, but also the Soul."*

~ Osho~

# CHAPTER 22

At the time of her induced coma, Leslie had a depleted system that included malnutrition, pneumonia, and MRSA: a generally fatal form of staph infection in her lungs.

However, while in her induced coma, she was making extraordinary progress. Her blood pressure was moving to normal, her high heart rate was normalizing, and her breathing capacity was increasing with each passing day. Her recovery was in full swing.

Although Leslie had been scheduled to be on the breathing machine for five days, overjoyed with her progress, her medical team decided to bring her out of her induced coma on the fourth day. Morti and I could hardly contain our sense of gratitude and excitement when that much anticipated morning arrived.

However, what her fabulous medical team and the rest of us had not counted on, was the reaction that all those drugs would have on her psyche. For Leslie, coming out of her induced coma was like awakening from a horrific nightmare in which the doctors, Morti and I, were the villains.

As she opened her eyes, Morti, Jaime, her favorite pulmonary therapist, and I, stood by her bed smiling down on her. Instead of smiling back at us like we expected, she looked around the room in absolute panic, and began pulling at her tubes while yelling hysterically at the top of her lungs. "*GET ME OUT OF HERE!*" The doctors succeeded in restraining her, but not before she had punched her attending physician and pulled the IV from her arm.

Restraining her made her even more angry and aggressive. As she struggled to break free, she yelled, "*GET AWAY FROM ME! GET AWAY FROM ME, YOU XXXXXXX. I AM NOT GOING TO LET YOU KILL ME! I RECOGNIZE ALL OF YOU! STAY THE XXXX AWAY FROM ME! I HAVE BEEN RUNNING AWAY FROM YOU ALL NIGHT.*

*I WON'T LET YOU KILL ME!*"

Since I had always been a calming influence for Leslie, I approached her bed and touched her tethered arm. Trying to calm her down, I smiled and said, *"Leslie Honey, you're back! You are okay now! Morti and I are here like we promised."*

Leslie looked up at me with terror in her eyes, and in a loud, threatening voice, shouted *"GET THE XXXX AWAY FROM ME! YOU ARE ONE OF THEM! Then she pointed to Morti and screamed, "YOU TWO WERE HELPING THEM TO KILL ME!"*

The whole scene had become much too weird for me. Had I believed in demons I would have thought that one of them had taken over my daughter's body. Shocked and very upset, I stepped back away from her reach.

Jaime, one of Leslie's favorite pulmonary therapists, who had asked to be present when she came out of her coma, looked very troubled when, using the *"F"* word, Leslie pointed to me and screamed, *"AND YOU, GET THE XXXX AWAY FROM ME!"*

*"LESLIE!"* Jaime called out to her assertively, *"don't talk to your mother like that!"* It was obvious that Jaime had not played a part in her nightmare because, at the sound of his voice, Leslie immediately stopped screaming at me and fixed her gaze on him. After giving Jaime her undivided attention, she silently

began scanning the room. Then, with a very puzzled look on her face, she asked, *"Where am I?"*

*"You're in an ICU room, Leslie,"* replied her doctor. Since she could not recall anything about the last four days, she asked, *"Why would I be in the ICU? Only sick people are in ICU rooms. I am very strong. Call Dr. Conrad, he'll tell you that I am one of his healthiest CF patients."*

No one, not even her attending physician, could convince Leslie that she was in the ICU. So, I suggested that we send for Linda, one of her favorite nurses. After a few moments, Linda walked into the ICU room and approached Leslie's bed.

Relieved to see her, Leslie said, *"Hi, Linda, I'm so glad you are here. Tell them how healthy and strong I am. Tell them I'm not sick enough for the ICU."*

Linda smiled as she gently touched Leslie's tethered arm. *"Leslie,"* she said, *"you are in the ICU. You went into respiratory arrest on Sunday and had to be put in an induced coma, and then on a breathing machine. Look around you Leslie, see all the machines. These are not in your regular room. You are in the ICU."*

Since, like Jaime, Linda had not been part of her nightmare, Leslie trusted her as well. In fact, in that ICU room that morning, Jaime and Linda were the only two people with whom Leslie felt safe.

Fortunately for Leslie, the drugs she had been given to induce the coma had an element of amnesia in them, which erased that Sunday afternoon crisis from her mind. Remembering nothing about the horrific day when her life had depended on being put into an induced coma and on a breathing machine, Leslie became quiet, and calmly listened to Linda.

Then, looking around the room at all the machines, in a soft, but confused tone, she said, *"This is not my regular room, it must be the ICU room. I've never been to the ICU before, and I still don't understand what I'm doing here."*

Noticing how calm Leslie seemed, the attending physician jumped on the opportunity to get the IV back into her arm. Leslie became extraordinarily cooperative as the doctor searched both arms for a good vein. Unable to find one in either arm, the doctor told Leslie that the IV had to be put in her groin. Again, she calmly agreed.

With a tight grip on Leslie's shoulders, the attending physician asked his young intern to begin the procedure. Leslie was quiet and restrained for a few more minutes. But, as soon as the intern began the procedure, she looked down at him and said, *"And don't you be looking at my boobs!"*

The handsome, young intern simply looked up at her and, in a very professional yet friendly tone, said, *"Trust me, Leslie, the last thing I'm thinking about right now is checking you out."* The scene was so surreal that it was difficult for Morti and me to keep from laughing.

Unfortunately, Leslie caught us. And thinking that we were laughing at her brought back all the fury that she had felt earlier. Pointing an accusing finger at me, she screamed, *"AND YOU, WHERE DID YOU GET THAT SWEATSHIRT? THAT IS MY SWEATSHIRT, TAKE IT OFF RIGHT NOW!"*

Then, when she spotted her "BELIEVE" necklace hanging around my neck, she had a total meltdown. Accusing me of stealing her necklace, she demanded that I take it off immediately and give it back. Trying to retrieve her stolen necklace, she attempted to sit up and reach for it. Fortunately, I had stepped away from her bed during the sweatshirt trauma and she was restrained before she could reach me. By now, it was all beginning to seem more like a scene in a Saturday Night Live episode than a hospital ICU room.

During that hysterical outburst, because we always borrowed things from each other, Leslie was telling the truth. I was wearing her sweatshirt and necklace.

I had spent the last four days with Morti at their home in San Diego and Just as I was getting into the car, I remembered how cold it was in the ICU room. So, I ran back into the house to borrow one of Leslie's sweatshirts. As I was pulling her *"BELIEVE"* sweatshirt over my head, I noticed her *"BELIEVE"* necklace on her dresser, and hung it around my neck.

I looked at my image in the mirror, and a chill ran down my back. *"The first thing she will see when she opens her eyes,"* I thought, *"will be the word BELIEVE, and it will remind her that believing is what brought her back to us."*

None of us took offense at any of it because we all knew it was not Leslie, but the drugs that were speaking and acting through her. It took about twelve hours for her to fully recover from her paranoiac reaction to the drugs that had kept her in a coma for four days.

That first night out of her induced coma was one of nightmares and frightening visions. Still suffering from drug-induced, acute paranoia, Leslie thought that every shadow and every person who entered her room, including her male nurse, was there to kill her.

The drama of her initial reaction to the drugs had been frightening yet amusing. But the most amazing insight for me that day, was the tremendous power that a drug-induced mind can have over the body.

Leslie had gone into her coma weighing 95 pounds, suffering from extreme malnutrition. With her lungs caked with mucus and infected with a deadly virus called MRSA, she was much too weak to even speak. Yet she came out of that induced coma screaming, demanding, accusing, and threatening with such incredible strength that it took two strong doctors to restrain her.

At first, as I witnessed the impossible happen, I kept asking myself, *"Where did Leslie get that kind of strength?"* Then suddenly, deep from the recesses of my mind, I got a powerful insight: just as her mind could be influenced by drugs to have incredible physical strength and power, her mind could be influenced by God's power of love to heal her.

*"What the caterpillar calls the end of the world the Master calls a butterfly."*

~ Richard Bach~

# CHAPTER 23

We all knew that the road back would not be easy, but none of us, especially Leslie, realized just how difficult it would be.

Although Leslie finally recovered from her extreme paranoia, she remained extremely weak and fearful. She had had lung treatments while in her coma, but her air passages were still so caked with mucus that even at high oxygen levels, she was still having trouble getting air to her lungs.

Although she didn't remember the Sunday episode in the ICU when she had been put into an induced coma and onto a breathing machine, she still carried the terrifying memory of waking up in the ICU room and not knowing why she was there.

Besides having been intravenously fed, Leslie had not eaten a real meal in over a week. So, she was too weak to feed herself or get in and out of bed without help. Besides that, she was also too emotionally and physically fragile to interact with, or even speak to our family, who sat silently in her darkened room.

Feeling extremely grateful that the terrible ordeal of the previous week was now behind us, all of us just sat there in the dark smiling at each other without uttering a single word.

After my Sunday service in Orange County, I headed for Thornton Hospital in La Jolla to be with Leslie. It was her first day out of ICU, and although she had slept most of the day, she seemed totally out of it. Absolutely exhausted, yet happy to see me, she reached out for my hand, and before falling into another deep sleep, she whispered, *"Hi, Mom. I'm glad you are here."* Holding her tiny hand in mine, I sat quietly by her bed for hours while she slept.

As Leslie slept, I looked across that darkened room and noticed that Morti looked very weary. So, I whispered, *"Morti, why don't you go home and get some sleep, and I'll spend the night with Leslie?"* He smiled, stood up, walked toward Leslie and kissed her lightly on the lips without waking her. Then, he squeezed my shoulder and slipped out of the darkened room with her brothers.

Leslie continued to sleep soundly for hours until her respiratory therapist arrived to give her a lung treatment. *"Leslie Honey,"* I whispered, *"you need to wake up. It's time for your treatment."*

Leslie slowly opened her eyes, looked up at the therapist's smiling face, and whispered a very weak *"Hello."* Although he was a substitute therapist that she did not know, she smiled warmly and thanked him for coming. The therapist carefully lifted Leslie's fragile body out of the bed and into a chair, then turned on the machine and began her treatment.

The ordeal of moving from the bed to a chair had left Leslie feeling so weak and exhausted that, as hard as she tried, she simply could not get air into her lungs. Terrified at her inability to breathe deeply, she began to cry.

As soon as the pulmonary therapist noticed the tears rolling down her cheeks, he turned off the machine and kneeled-down before her. Holding her tiny, trembling hands in his, he acknowledged her fear. Then, in an extremely warm and personal way, he reassured her that she would eventually get her strength back. *"After all,"* he said to her, *"you have just come off a breathing machine, you are still very weak. Your body just needs time to adjust and heal."*

Then he reminded her of the importance of a positive attitude during this period of recovery. As an aside, he mentioned the power of positive thinking that he had recently learned at a Unity church. At the mention of Unity, Leslie's eyes brightened. She smiled and told him that her mother was a Unity minister.

As soon as he noticed that Leslie was breathing more easily, the therapist turned on the machine and finished the treatment. Then he carried Leslie back to her bed, smiled at both of us, shook my hand and left the room.

Thrilled at how much better she seemed after her interaction with that insightful therapist, I had a folding cot brought into her room so I could spend the night with her.

We had both been asleep for an hour when I heard her gasping for air again. I jumped out of my cot, got into her bed, held her hand and quietly affirmed one of my favorite passages from A Course in Miracles: *"Spirit are you, Leslie honey,"* I affirmed, *"safe and whole and healed."* I continued to affirm that again and again, until she began to breathe easier and finally fell asleep.

I never returned to my cot. Although neither of us got much sleep that night, on a level that neither of us recognized at the time, the power of love had lifted us higher. And although Leslie and I had always had a close relationship, I had never felt as connected to her as I did that morning.

Still holding hands when we awoke, there was such a deep feeling of connection between us that neither of us felt like getting up. Lying together in her small, hospital bed we talked for over an hour about so many things.

Leslie thanked me for spending the night with her and told me how much she loved and appreciated me. We reminisced about her younger years, and she asked me to forgive her for having been a difficult teenager. *"I love you, Mom! I'm so sorry I was so mean to you when I was a teenager,"* she said. I thanked her for having chosen me to be her mom this time around, and we laughed and cried together as we recalled many good times, and some painful ones.

Our reverie was interrupted by a loud knock on her hospital room door. "Come in," called Leslie. Annoyed at the interruption, I jumped out of her bed and moved toward the open door where a nurse with a wheelchair was standing. *Leslie,* said the nurse, *"I am here to take you downstairs for a quick procedure. You need to have the IV removed from your groin and put back in your arm."*

Knowing that it was a simple procedure that Leslie had endured dozens of times before, I suggested that I return to Brea where I had lots of work piled up. *"This is a simple procedure, Mom,"* she assured me. *"I won't be gone for over thirty minutes. Please wait until I get back and we'll have lunch together before you leave."* After that meaningful night and morning together, I couldn't pull myself away either. So, I agreed to wait.

As the nurse wheeled Leslie out of her room, I sat in her recliner, made myself comfortable and reached for my book. Knowing how difficult it was to find a good vein in Leslie's arm, I was still not concerned, when an hour had passed, and Leslie had not returned to her room.

At that point, I decided to go to the cafeteria for a cup of coffee and continue reading there. Time passes very quickly for me when I'm reading a good book. So, when I looked down at my watch and noticed that another two hours had gone by, I jumped up and headed for the exit sign above the cafeteria entrance. Thinking that Leslie would be impatiently waiting for me, when I got off the elevator, I ran all the way to her room.

As I approached her room, I noticed two men moving her bed toward the door. *"What are you doing?"* I shouted. *"Why are you moving my daughter's bed out of her room?"*

*"Sorry, lady,"* said one of them, *"we are just following orders."* Frustrated, confused, and desperately trying to find someone who could help me, I ran to the front desk.

Crazy with anxiety, I screamed at the nurse behind the counter. *"I'M LESLIE PETRONE'S MOTHER!* ***PLEASE, PLEASE STOP THOSE MEN FROM MOVING MY DAUGHTERS BED OUT OF HER ROOM!"***

Totally spent from all that drama, I managed to calm down to a moment of restored sanity and muttered, *"My daughter Leslie is just having a simple procedure that usually doesn't take more than half an hour, and she should be back in her room by now."* Then, *in a very loud, trembling voice I asked, "WHERE IS SHE? WHY ISN'T SHE BACK?"*

The fear and anxiety behind my question was so obvious that the head nurse quickly stepped out from behind the counter. In a gentle but clear voice, she said, *"I'm sorry, Reverend Johnson, we are moving Leslie's bed out because that is no longer her room. "Leslie is back in ICU! She went into respiratory arrest during the procedure, and had to be put back on a respirator."* My heart sank! I could hardly believe my ears. Remembering that respirators can destroy lung tissue, I panicked at the thought of Leslie being back on that machine for a second time. *"**Oh No!**"* I gasped. *"It can't be true. She can't be back on that machine. No! No! Please God, tell me this is not happening. She was doing so well this morning!"*

Filled with anxiety, I found myself reliving the poignant moments Leslie and I had shared that very morning. There had been such a meaningful sense of connection between us as we talked, reminisced, laughed and cried together, that we planned to continue that conversation when she returned from her procedure.

Instead of giving me some level of comfort, those warm, meaningful memories now made me so sad that I began torturing myself with thoughts like, *"does this mean she is not going to recover? Did she say all those things to me this morning because, on some level, she knew she was going to die? Maybe I was dumb to believe in the miracle that the Peruvian shaman had promised."*

As one fear-based thought followed another, I found myself in a very dark place emotionally. The tears were gushing down my throat so fast, I couldn't catch my breath. I rubbed my eyes trying desperately to scrub away the flood of tears that seemed to be drowning me. Soon, I felt like I was standing in a puddle of water that kept rising. It wasn't raining, the water was coming from me. Although I did everything I possibly could to regain my composure, I simply could not stop sobbing.

After an hour, the tears stopped long enough to enable me to clear my sore throat, blow my nose and call Morti at work. *"Morti,"* I cried, *"you need to get over here immediately! Leslie is back in ICU. She had a simple procedure and went into respiratory arrest! She is in another induced coma and back on a respirator. I'm heading toward ICU as we speak. Please hurry!"*

As I walked back into that ICU room for the second time and saw Leslie on that respirator, I really didn't have a clue what this second time around was all about. However, what I did know was that allowing fear to take over could destroy everything that we had managed to co-create during the previous week.

At the time, no other woman with cystic fibrosis in the history of Thornton Hospital, had ever survived a week on a respirator. And this was Leslie's second time. Those facts triggered a feeling of terror in my soul that threatened to overwhelm me all over again.

In the middle of all that emotional turmoil, a powerful question popped into my mind. *Could this be another premeditated gift that I am free to accept or reject?* As I pondered that question, I felt those goosebumps run up and down my spine that always confirmed the truth for me. So, in spite of my apprehensions, I accepted the second induced coma and respirator as another premeditated gift, and placed my trust again, in God's healing power deep within Leslie. Regardless of the circumstances, I decided that I would not allow fear to stop the good that was trying to happen for Leslie.

Morti and I put all the same procedures in place that we had during Leslie's first induced coma, only this time we allowed her brothers to be in her room. Also, remembering her reaction to the drugs in her first induced coma, Leslie was given a smaller dose the second time around.

However, the problem with reducing the dosage was that, at times, appearing to be awake, she would open her eyes and point to the window. Intent on making her comfortable, her brother Russ would open the window and say, *"I guess you need some fresh air."*

Then she would point to the ceiling and Tom would laugh and say, *"okay Les, we got it. It must be too bright in here for you."* And he would turn off the lights, only to have her point to the window again. Trying to figure out what she wanted filled the room with joy and laughter. That is, until she tried to pull the breathing tube out of her mouth and had to be restrained and given a higher dose.

Leslie was doing so well this second time, that her doctor decided to bring her out of this second, induced coma in just three days. And with his assurance that this time things would be better, I left the hospital on Friday night and headed for Orange County to prepare for my Sunday service.

On Saturday morning, Leslie's doctor, Morti and her brothers were standing by her bed waiting for

Leslie to awaken from her coma. Much to their relief, with no drama whatsoever, Leslie opened her eyes, looked around the room and smiled.

Despite her physical struggles, Leslie always managed to remain open and vulnerable and allowed the life force to lift her as high as she could rise. It was that attitude and her meaningful relationship with Morti, that moved her forty-three years beyond her original prognosis of dying at age seven.

I had just finished preparing my Sunday Lesson when the phone rang. As I reached for the phone, my heart was pounding so fast that I thought it would skip a beat. *"Hello,"* I said with a bit of trepidation. My son Tom answered the phone and, in a very upbeat voice, he said *"Hello Mother!"*

Before Tom could utter another word, I asked, *"How is Leslie?"*

Ignoring my question, he simply said, *"There is someone here who wants to talk to you,"* and he handed the phone to his sister.

And, as far as I was concerned at the time, after saying "Hi Mom," Leslie uttered the two most wonderful words on the planet. ***"I'm back!"***

*"I am receptive to the inflow and outpouring of the Universe."*

~Eric Butterworth~

# CHAPTER 24

My congregation in Brea was extremely accommodating to the crazy schedule that Leslie's illness created in their minister's life. One Sunday after the service, a member whom I loved and respected called me aside and suggested that I should consider living closer to Leslie. *"As much as I hate the thought of losing you as my minister, Dr. Julie,"* she said, *"a mother should be near her sick child. You need to move to San Diego and be near your daughter. She needs to have you close by."*

Although I had hashed and rehashed the subject of moving to San Diego in the past, the realization that Leslie could be taken from me suddenly, had really convinced me that I should live near her.

As we were getting ready to put Leslie in an induced coma and on a respirator in that ICU room, I had promised myself that when Leslie made it through that crisis, I would move to San Diego and help with her recovery. So, my friend's suggestion, which seemed to confirm my conscious choice, touched me deeply.

Once I set my intention on living closer to Leslie, my condo in Brea, which I had really enjoyed decorating, lost all its charm for me. So, I placed it on the market and sold it in two weeks. Trusting in more Divine Order, I found a condo to rent in San Diego and hired movers to get me there.

The movers, had arrived early and were busy loading the truck when my son Russ, who was my real estate agent, called to tell me that my condo had fallen out of escrow. At first, I could not understand how such a set-back could occur when everything had been flowing in such Divine Order.

Disappointed and confused, my egoic mind wanted me to stop the movers and stay in Brea. Then I remembered that some of the worst things that seemed to happen to me always resulted in wonderful outcomes. So, I made the decision to keep moving forward and told the movers to keep on loading the truck. Then I put the condo up for rent.

Weeks after moving to San Diego, I got a call from the president of the board of trustees of the Unity Church of Carlsbad, a suburb of San Diego. *"We are in the middle of a job search for a new senior minister,* she said, *and I think you should apply."*

Excited at how quickly the universe had provided what I needed after I had honored my commitment, I sent a resume, had an interview, and got the job.

Although, on a conscious level at the time, I didn't know that I only had four years left with my precious girl, I'll always be grateful that there was a deeper part of me that did.

*"The key to abundance is meeting limited circumstances with unlimited thoughts."*

~ Marianne Williamson~

# CHAPTER 25

Shortly after retiring at age forty, Leslie created her own fundraising team called the Caring Friends Team. At first, the team consisted only of her family and a few friends who started with tee shirts on which Leslie had written *"Believe"* with a sharpie pen. The team eventually grew to over seven hundred donors, becoming one of the top-grossing cystic fibrosis teams in the nation and raising over $500,000.00 for a cure.

Every year, during the month of May, Leslie and her team held a CF WALK in San Diego, where family and friends came together to walk and donate for a cure. After each WALK, many of us went to Leslie's home to celebrate. Even though she was feeling extremely weak in May of 2011, Leslie hosted a party for over 60 people who had donated over $90,000.00 to her CF WALK.

After every CF WALK, Leslie wrote a heartfelt Thank-You letter to her committed donors. As she approached her fiftieth birthday, she wrote, *"Staying healthy this year became a full-time job, leaving little time for enjoying life, and I truly began to lose HOPE. My shift in attitude finally came when I realized how much I had to be grateful for. I was told that I would not live to be 7 years old, and this year I will celebrate my 50th birthday! As a person with cystic fibrosis, a devastating disease, I am 43 years over my life expectancy…a privilege that I do not take lightly. That is why I have devoted a decade of my life to making a difference for CF. I am living proof that what we do together directly impacts my quality of life every day."*

At her last party, Leslie's good friend Stacy Motenko, who also had cystic fibrosis, invited Leslie to attend her CF WALK in Orange County in June of 2011. Leslie agreed to go but when the time arrived, she didn't feel strong enough to go alone and invited me to go with her.

As usual, Leslie grabbed my keys and sat in the driver's seat. As we drove to Orange County, I noticed how tired she looked and asked her if she was okay. She replied that she had been feeling very tired all week and this time, she simply could not rise above it.

When we finally arrived at the park where Stacy was hosting her CF WALK, Leslie felt too weak to get out of the car without my help. Her energy level was so low, that as we walked ever so slowly, she asked if we could stop at a large tree and rest for a few minutes.

Walking arm in arm, we finally reached the park and approached the stage where Stacy was standing. As soon as Stacy spotted Leslie, she asked her to come up to the microphone and speak to the crowd. Despite her low energy and the dark circles under her eyes that made her look exceptionally tired, Leslie spoke enthusiastically to the crowd about the importance of raising money for a cure for cystic fibrosis.

When we finally joined the group on the CF WALK, Leslie was having trouble keeping up even though they were walking rather slowly. "*Slow down, Mom,*" she said. "*I'm having trouble catching my breath.*"

After the event, as we were walking to the car, she squeezed my arm and said, "*Mom, would you please drive us home. I'm feeling too sick to drive.*" At first, I simply could not believe my ears. Leslie always insisted on driving whenever we drove together in my car. Even as sick and weak as she had felt when we arrived in Tucson, Arizona ten years earlier, Leslie had insisted on driving the twenty miles from the airport to Dr. Weil's office. So, her suggestion that I drive, really frightened and upset me.

By July of that year, Leslie was in the hospital. On August 15, still in the ICU room, she celebrated her fiftieth birthday with family, friends, doctors and a staff who loved her. Shortly after her fiftieth birthday celebration, Leslie was in the USC Transplant Center, waiting for a new set of lungs.

Although, at that point, everyone was praying for a new set of lungs for Leslie. The operation was postponed again and again due to her low-grade fever and inflammation issues.

Taking care of Leslie became Morti's full-time job. He never left her side. Getting little sleep and often skipping meals, he practically lived in her room. As her advocate, he learned her routine, monitored her medications, and became as knowledgeable about her condition as any respiratory therapist.

Once I asked Morti who had been by Leslie's side 24/7 in her ICU room for three months, "knowing what you know now, would you have married her?

"Absolutely!" was his immediate reply. "I wouldn't have missed the last nineteen years with her for anything."

As Leslie became too weak to talk, she began to motion for what she needed. One day, as I was standing by her bed with Morti, she motioned that she needed more oxygen. Morti immediately told the respiratory therapist, who was also standing there, to increase Leslie's oxygen supply. Using her authority as a pulmonary therapist, she told him that Leslie was getting all the oxygen she needed.

Fiercely protective of his beloved wife, Morti stared at the therapist with fire in his eyes for a minute or so before exploding. Then, in a loud voice that even frightened me who had never experienced him that way. He said, *"GIVE HER ALL THE OXYGEN SHE WANTS RIGHT NOW!"*

Shocked and noticeably upset, the therapist, who obviously knew not to mess with a lion committed to taking care of her cub, immediately increased Leslie's oxygen level, turned toward the door and quickly left the room.

*"Even when clouds grow thick, the sun still pours its light earthward."*

~ Mark Nepo~

# CHAPTER 26

By September of 2011, Leslie was still in the transplant center in Los Angeles, waiting for a pair of lungs. She seemed very excited about the prospect of new lungs when I left her and headed for home that day.

My brother Bill's daughter Joann, the cousin who played with Leslie in her oxygen tent when they were both little girls, had just flown into town to go to her father's 80th birthday celebration with me the next day.

We were having an early dinner, when suddenly all the lights in the house went out. I ran outside to see if any of my neighbors were experiencing the same thing, and soon discovered that Southern California was having a **blackout.**

I was frantically searching through the house for a flashlight when the phone rang. It was Morti. Sounding very scared, he said, *"Julie, can you come back immediately? Things look bad for Leslie. She is non-responsive, and I'm afraid that she may not make it through the night."*

Fighting back my tears, I said, *"Oh, Morti, that is so hard to believe. She seemed so well when I left her this afternoon. Please hold on, I'll be there as soon as possible."*

With an aching heart, I hung up the phone, grabbed my dog Lexie, and raced across the street to my dog sitter's house. Lexie, who had been a gift from Leslie three years earlier, was an exact replica of my dog Alex, a Cavalier King Charles Spaniel whose image hung on my wall.

One day, Leslie called and told me that her friend was searching for a good home for a beautiful puppy. My initial reaction was that I wasn't ready for another dog.

However, the minute I held her, I knew that I had found my next dog. And It didn't take long for Lexie to become Leslie's dog away from home.

Once my dog sitter agreed to keep Lexie overnight, Joann and I headed for the Los Angeles Freeway, where we were about to experience one of the most frightening night's of our lives.

The lack of lights, both on the streets and the freeway, was not only scary but very, dangerous. Besides having to swing around some accidents and stopped cars, we were forced to drive very slowly for long stretches of highway, or drive very fast, bumper to bumper in the dark.

It took four hours to get from Orange County to the USC Medical Transplant Center in Los Angeles, and another thirty minutes to find a parking space once we were there. At 12:30 PM, four and a half hours after receiving the summons from Morti, I finally arrived at Leslie's ICU room.

Her nurse, who greeted me at the door, told me that things didn't look good for Leslie. She was having trouble breathing and the carbon dioxide was building in her brain. In fact, she said in a very compassionate voice, *"She may not make it through the night."*

In a state of panic at the thought of losing Leslie without saying goodbye, I pulled up a chair and sat by her bed. Since her eyes were closed, I couldn't tell if she was sleeping or unconscious. So, I simply took her hand in mine, and sat there thinking about how very fortunate I was to have been chosen to walk this life-time with her. We had accomplished so much and had come so far: farther than either of us could have imagined. Perhaps the time had come to let her go, I thought. But I was just not ready to lose her.

Since Leslie had not had enough energy to talk for weeks, whenever she needed to say something, she would just mouth it to us. Much to my surprise, after about twenty minutes, Leslie opened her eyes, looked at me and mouthed, *"Hi, Mama!"*

Hoping she wouldn't notice how scared I felt, I simply smiled and said, *"Hi, Leslie Honey."* I'm not sure why I always called her *"Leslie honey."* Although I always called her brothers "honey," for some reason that I can't explain, I always connected her name to that endearing term.

As we smiled at each other, her cousin Joann, whom I had left in the lobby, entered the room. Although Leslie seemed quite pleased to see her, instead of bubbling over with affection for her cousin as she always had, Joann seemed very aloof. Sensing this, Leslie kept trying to say the word *"telephone,"* but just could not get it out.

As it turned out, before Leslie got so sick, she used to spend hours talking to her cousin Joann and to her friends on her cell phone. However, a few weeks before she entered the hospital, she noticed that talking required more energy than she had to spare. So, It had become very, difficult for her to spend long periods of time chatting on the phone with her friends.

*"Mom,"* she said one day, *"I'm not calling you as often as usual because It just takes too much energy to talk on the phone anymore. And the worst part,"* she continued, *"is that my friends and Joann can't understand why I'm not returning their calls."*

*"Maybe you should tell them that you no longer have enough energy for long conversations,"* I suggested. But, convinced that she would soon bounce back as she had always done in the past, Leslie refused to do that. And eventually, the inevitable happened. Joann kept calling and instead of telling her how she was feeling, Leslie just refused to take her calls. Feeling weak, scared, and frustrated, the next time Joann called, Leslie picked up the phone and said, *"Joann, I can't talk right now. Please stop stalking me!"* Then, before she could explain, Joann hung up and they had not spoken since.

Slowing dying from carbon dioxide poisoning, Leslie was desperately trying to explain why she had spoken to Joann that way. But as hard as she tried, the only word she could form with her mouth was *"telephone, telephone,"* which she muttered in a very, low whisper.

Knowing about their previous altercation, I explained to Joann that Leslie was trying to make amends. Feeling justifiably hurt, Joann hesitated for a few minutes before hugging Leslie and assuring her that she was forgiven.

Satisfied with her amends, Leslie then turned to me and with tears streaming down her face, said, *"Mom, I want to go. I've only stayed for Morti and you. But now I need to go. Please help me to go. I know you can do it. Please, please help me to go!"*

The pain that I felt at that moment was so intense that I had trouble responding. *"No, you can't leave now,"* I thought. *"What about the new lungs that are coming soon?"*

So many thoughts were running through my head at that moment, that It took a minute or so, before I could form a response. Finally, I said, *"Okay!"* Then, as I tightened my grip on her hand, I whispered, *"Leslie, I'll help you with this, if you promise that you will come to me once you are in the spirit world."* She nodded *"YES!"* And, before we closed our eyes to pray, with great difficulty she mouthed three words. *"If I can."*

Although I prayed with Leslie that night, I simply could not give her The Last Rites. Instead, convinced that a pair of new lungs was the highest and best for her, I asked God to guide Leslie's spirit to her highest good. As we opened our eyes, the nurse, who was standing there checking Leslie's vitals, smiled at her, and said, *"Leslie you are much better!"* Then she bent down to me and whispered, *"I think she might make it through the night."*

It was 3:00 AM before Joann and I found a suitable hotel in LA and got settled in for the night. The next day, awake at 8:00 AM, we rushed back to Leslie's ICU room. To our delight, we found her sitting up in bed, looking well and happy.

Feeling thrilled to the bone with her progress, I believed that her spirit had chosen to stay.

With the blackout over, we headed for San Diego to share the good news at the family reunion.

While she was waiting for her lungs, Leslie had days when her temperature was normal and she felt wonderful. And, she had days when her inflammation was at an all-time high. I was standing by her bed on one of those good days when the doctor came in and said, *"Leslie, it should just be a matter of weeks before you get your new lungs."*

Thrilled with the good news, but too weak to speak, she raised her hands over her head, giving her doctor a "thumbs up," and mouthed *"thank you!"*

*"Don't thank me, Leslie,"* said the doctor. *"Thank yourself for working so hard."* With tears running down her cheeks, she gave him a dazzling smile.

I, on the other hand, could not control my need to express gratitude. *"THANK YOU, GOD!"* I shouted before spontaneously reaching across the bed to grab the doctor's hand. *"Thank you, Doctor! Thank you, Doctor!"* I repeated.

Once the doctor confirmed the arrival of a new pair of lungs, I emailed everyone I knew with the good news and asked them to pray for the perfect match. Finally, a week after all those prayers went out, a set of lungs arrived. Unfortunately, Leslie's antibodies were not a good match for them. Luckily, a week later, another pair of lungs arrived, but Leslie had a fever, so she could not have the operation.

After losing that second set of lungs, Leslie's enthusiasm about the transplant waned, and she began to slowly slip away.

*"One day it happens. The inexorable thing that you have feared all your life. But you're never ready."*

~ Marie Howe~

# CHAPTER 27

It was Thursday morning in Los Angeles, and Leslie's brother Russ and I had come to The USC Medical Transplant Center to spend the day with her.

As we entered Leslie's ICU room, we were both shocked and saddened by the huge change that had taken place in her condition. Just a few days earlier, her friend Kasey had arrived with a stylist to wash, trim and style Leslie's long hair. They made Leslie look beautiful, and she seemed so happy and alert throughout the entire procedure, that they decided to return the following week.

And today, only three days later, tears filled my son's eyes as he approached his sister's bed, smiled, and said his usual *"Hi, honey."* Leslie, who was always excited to see Russ, looked past him as if he were not there.

Because Leslie could no longer sit up in bed, during her last three weeks at the transplant center, she would be strapped onto a table that could be turned upright so that she could hug us when we came to visit.

Noticing the pained expression on my face, Leslie's occupational therapist, Nicole, with her usual smile, had my sweet girl moved from her bed to the portable table, saying, *"Leslie, lets strap you to the table so you can stand up and give your mother a big hug before she leaves for Tahiti for your brother's wedding."*

Nicole, a marvelous therapist who seemed to brighten Leslie's spirit whenever she entered her room, got no reaction from Leslie that day. Although she had always reacted to Nicole's voice with a nod and happy grin, this time it seemed as if Leslie had not heard a single word that Nicole had spoken. With tears in her eyes, Nicole strapped Leslie's limp body to the table and placed her in a standing position.

Without any hesitation, I wrapped my arms around my beloved daughter. However today, although she gave it a courageous try, Leslie was unable to wrap her arms around me as she had always done. Using every bit of will power that she could muster, Leslie tried to lift her arms, but before they reached my back, they fell limply to her sides. Then, she made a second attempt with the same results. Refusing to give up, Leslie attempted to lift her arms for a third time. This time, she was able to lift them high enough to touch my back before they limply fell to her sides.

Refusing to let go of her, I just stood there with my arms tightly wrapped around Leslie's fragile body. Somehow, realizing that she was unable to hug me, Leslie moved her face toward mine, and gently kissed me on each cheek before returning to her blank stare.

As painful as that moment was, I knew on a very deep level, that Leslie was saying *"Goodbye, Mom!"* As it eventually played out, that kiss on each cheek turned out to be our final farewell.

After that emotional experience, I felt torn between being there for Leslie and officiating at my son's wedding in Tahiti. Leslie was scheduled for dialysis the next day, and her nurse, who assured me that sometimes patients bounced back when the toxins were removed from their body, gave me the needed courage to leave my daughter and be there for my son.

Russ, who adored his sister, had always lovingly allowed her and her illness to take center stage in our lives. Knowing that in the Tahitian, civil wedding ceremony, the presence of Mothers was paramount, and understanding the importance of this moment in my son Russell's life, I left Leslie and boarded a plane for Tahiti.

Everything about the wedding in Tahiti seemed wonderful. From the moment the hula dancers welcomed us at the airport, we knew that something meaningful was waiting to happen. And, something wonderful did happen! Leslie's spirit left her body in California and joined us there.

On October 11, 2011, Russell and Kathleen had three wedding ceremonies. The first, was a civil wedding at the mayor's office. Facing the couple, the mayor, speaking in French with an English-speaking interpreter, made the marriage official. Since the Tahitian custom for this ceremony was to celebrate motherhood, the bride and groom were seated at a table with their mothers beside them: Kathleen's mother sat next to her, and I was seated next to my son Russ.

While the Civil wedding was performed in an air-conditioned, court house, the traditional, Tahitian and English ceremonies took place on the beach. Without the slightest breeze to keep us cool, the hot sun was mercilessly shining down on all of us. Yet, we were all so thrilled to be celebrating

Russell's first wedding at age 48, and Kathleen's at age 36, that we gladly endured that day's all-consuming heat and humidity.

Before the English ceremony began, Kathleen asked us to form a large circle. Then in order to create a sacred space, she placed two flat rocks with the word LOVE written in the center of each one, on the sand in front of her. Then, holding up a silver heart with the word LOVE at its center, Kathleen explained that it belonged to Leslie. And we were to symbolically include Leslie by passing the silver heart around the circle. As Leslie's silver heart passed from person to person in that circle, each of us held it tightly for a few seconds, and said a silent prayer before handing it to the next person.

Since I was the officiant, the heart came to me last. As I stood there with my daughter's silver heart in my hand, Leslie's presence was so palpable that it moved me to tears. And as I looked around the circle, I noticed that many were having the same reaction.

Feeling that the two "love" rocks represented the healing power of love that was moving through Leslie at the time, I threw the silver heart into the sand, hoping it would land next to them.

Disappointed, I noticed that Leslie's "love" heart landed face down, quite a distance from two rocks. Disappointed with the outcome, I turned my attention away from the silver heart and began the wedding ceremony.

After I had pronounced Russell and Kathleen, husband and wife and they had sealed their vows with a kiss, In a very emotional tone, Kathleen exclaimed, *"LOOK WHAT LESLIE DID TO THE HEART!*

We all looked in the direction of the silver heart, and astonished, we noticed that although there had not been the slightest breeze, Leslie's silver heart lay right-side-up in the sand right next to the other two rocks. Then, to make the whole experience even more mystical, the camera that was set on automatic to film that ceremony was blank. Unable to capture the seeming impossible, the camera had stopped filming. Even though at that point, I was still unaware that Leslie's spirit had already left her body, I knew, without a doubt, that we had felt her presence.

Meanwhile, early that morning, back in California, the dialysis had left Leslie with very little brain activity. And, her doctor had told Morti that it was time to take her off life support. *"How long will it take her to die once we take her off life support?"* Grief stricken Morti asked her doctor.

*"Most people stop breathing in one to two hours,"* he sadly replied.

At first, Morti did not think he was capable of removing Leslie from life-support, but with the love and encouragement of Louann, one of Leslie's best friends, Morti found the strength and courage to make that very difficult decision.

Once the assistive devices were removed, Leslie left as she had lived—on her own terms. In just ten minutes, her spirit departed from her body peacefully without so much as a gasp for breath. After all, she had a wedding to attend in Tahiti.

Surprised at how quickly it happened, Morti refused to leave her. Crying inconsolably, with Leslie's tiny hand resting in his, he sat next to the love of his life for a very long time.

*"The wound is the place where the light enters you."*

~ Rumi~

# CHAPTER 28

After breakfast the next morning, Russell handed me a note that said to call Eric. *"Perhaps Eric was just calling to congratulate you on your wedding,"* I said to my newly married son. Then, as our eyes locked, I knew that something more ominous had happened back in California.

With great trepidation, I put a call through to the USA. Eric, who had not come to the wedding, answered the phone. *"Hi, Mom,"* he said. *"I have bad news. Leslie passed yesterday on the early morning of Russ's wedding day."*

At first, the fact that Leslie had died on her brother's wedding day was not much comfort to me. However, it didn't take long to realize that Leslie, who adored her brother, chose to begin her new experience in living on the same day that Russ and Kathleen were beginning theirs as husband and wife.

Despite the deep sadness they felt in losing her, Russ and Kathleen felt so honored that Leslie had chosen their wedding day to leave this plane of existence, that they kept her ashes vowing to celebrate her life on each of their anniversaries.

Many wonderful plans were crushed with that five-minute phone call to Eric. For example, my son Tom, who had planned to introduce the woman he was with as his new wife in a more elaborate fashion, had to blurt it out to me as I was boarding the bus to the airport.

*"Mom,"* he announced, *"I was married two weeks ago, and not wanting to rain on Russ and Kathleen's parade, I waited until we got to Tahiti to tell you."*

At that moment, I was too shocked and miserable to process anymore information. So, as I was boarding the bus to the airport, my only response to Tom's wedding announcement was *"WHAT?"*

That long trip back from Tahiti to California was horrendous. It was impossible to imagine a world without Leslie. It felt like a huge, gaping hole had just been dug in my heart, and there was nothing I could do to reduce the galvanizing pain. My indescribable sense of grief and loss in a mind that was spinning with unanswered questions, made me want to die as well.

The main question that kept cycling through my head was, "*why didn't she wait for me?*" As I obsessed about her passing, I kept asking myself if her final exit had been painful and long or quick and painless as I had always promised her that it would be.

Sick with grief about having to live in a world without Leslie, while hashing and rehashing that mind boggling question, I didn't sleep a wink that night. It was almost morning before the answer finally appeared; Leslie, who loved her family and adored her brother, wanted to be at his wedding. And leaving a body that had her spirit trapped for such a long time, was the only way she could do that.

As soon as I arrived in California, hoping to share that good news with Morti and get some answers to the many questions that were still flooding my grief-stricken mind, I called him. Unfortunately for me at the time, crazy with grief over losing Leslie, Morti had turned off his cell phone and could not be reached.

Frantic, instead of calling my son Eric, who was waiting to give me a ride home from the airport, I took a taxi to my condo in San Diego. Minutes after arriving home alone, I regretted my decision.

As a symbol of love and protection, Leslie had hung a Peace Angel next to my front door, where it still hangs. But that day, as I walked through the door alone and looked up at the angel of peace, I felt very, very little, if any, peace.

Reminders of Leslie were everywhere. Photographs testifying to my unbearable loss, hung on the walls in every room. There were pictures of Leslie with her brothers and me at their weddings, at her CF WALKS, at family gatherings, at their college graduations; all of them painfully exacerbating my unbearable sense of loss.

Trying to ignore the galvanizing pain in my gut, I decided to unpack. I carried my suitcase into the bedroom and reached for a pair of shoes. At first, holding those shoes in my hands filled me with happy memories of the days we had shopped until we had almost dropped. Those happy memories soon changed into a state of unbearable sadness that had me choking on my tears.

The leather desk cover and pen holder sitting on my desk, were Christmas gifts that reminded me of her. In my bathroom hung a shower curtain and towels she had put there when decorating my new condo. That treadmill and the Lexus that we had purchased together, stood as silent reminders of her thoughtful and generous spirit.

The treadmill was to keep me in shape, and the Lexus was to keep me safe. Her directive was clear! *"Now that you are an experienced, freeway driver, you need a car that will keep you safe. So I'm going to find the perfect, used Lexus in your price bracket, in a color that you like."* And she did!

I sank into the couch that sat in front of the armoire I had purchased from her when I moved into my condo. Everywhere I looked, I saw painful reminders of my one-of-a-kind daughter whose presence would no longer color my world.

Overwhelmed with memories of Leslie, I cried with an ache in my heart that seemed to be sucking the life out of me. Then all of a sudden, Eric came to mind, and I remembered that I hadn't called him. So I picked up my cell phone to dial his number and I noticed that I had a saved message from Leslie.

*"Mom,"* said the voice on my phone, *"you don't have to call me back. I just wanted to tell you that I'm sorry I haven't been able to spend much time with you lately. It's not because I don't want to. I love you and really enjoy being with you......."*

Convinced that hearing her voice meant that she was not really gone, I listened and listened. Despite the pain and feelings of abandonment that listening to her voice on my phone triggered in me, I simply could not stop. Instead of reminding me of the wonderful life we had shared, all these reminders, especially her voice, which sounded just like mine, reminded me of her absence.

Just as I felt like I would die of a broken heart, the phone rang. It was my son Eric, wanting to know how I had gotten home and why I hadn't called him to pick me up at the airport.

*"How are you feeling, Mom?"* he asked.

*"Oh, Eric,"* I cried. *"She is everywhere I look. This house is full of Leslie's energy, and instead of reminding me of her wonderful presence, it reminds me that I will have to live without her. How am I going to do that, Eric? I can't do it, I just can't. I don't want to live in a world without Leslie!"*

Eric tried his best to support and comfort me, but having never seen his mother so distraught, he just didn't know what to do or say. And, since Leslie, who was twelve years older, had always felt more like a mother than a sister to him, his own grief and terrible sense of loss made it difficult for him to be of much comfort to me.

Needing to be alone with the sound of her voice, I refused to answer the phone or speak to anyone. For almost a week, with neurotic regularity, I listened and listened and listened to her voice on my cell phone.

For the first time in my life, I was having mood swings that moved me from a deep sense of sadness and denial to extreme anger. As I looked at her picture and listened to her voice, I would beg her not to leave me and tell her that I simply did not want to live without her. An hour later, I was angrily screaming at her picture. *"You talked me into selling my house in Brea and moving to San Diego just to be near you, AND NOW YOU HAVE ABANDONED ME HERE!"*

Soon Saturday rolled around and it was time to give my Sunday Lesson. Although I could have found a guest speaker, I convinced myself that I needed to comfort my congregation, who really loved Leslie. And to make matters worse, I thought that giving the Sunday Lesson myself, would be a distraction from the pain that seemed to be breaking me open; WRONG!!!!

Five minutes into my sermon about the mystery of death, my lips began to tremble and my eyes teared up. Somehow, I managed to finish my lesson, but I doubt that my congregation heard any of it. Their sadness about losing Leslie and their love and compassion for me, just got in the way.

*"We live in a world alive with holy moments. We need only take the time to bring these moments into the light."*

~ Kent Nerburn~

# CHAPTER 29

Leslie had an incredible sense of style that her brothers and I really trusted. I especially relied on it whenever I needed to purchase an outfit for a special occasion. Consequently, purchasing a dress for her memorial service without Leslie, who was an expert at picking out clothes and colors that looked exceptionally good on me, was almost impossible.

As hard as I tried to focus on the task at hand, I kept hearing her voice in my head saying, *"No, not that one Mom, wrong color,"* or *"It doesn't look good on you. Try this one instead."* So, it was no surprise that after hours of searching in Leslie's favorite department store for the perfect outfit for her celebration of life service, I left the store empty handed.

Words are truly inadequate to describe the anxiety that gripped my soul when I decided to officiate at my daughter's service. Russell Senior, Leslie's birth dad, suggested that officiating at our daughter's memorial service would keep me from processing my own sense of grief. I knew there was some truth in that, but I also knew that, besides being her mother, I was Leslie's favorite minister. And, after a fifty-year journey through the world of cystic

227

fibrosis with her, there was no doubt in my mind that she would have wanted me to do it.

Morti and I spent days looking for a church in which to have Leslie's service. Because Leslie loved beauty, we knew the church had to be beautiful. And, because she was so loved, we knew the church had to be spacious. During our search, we found lots of beautiful churches. Unfortunately, many of them only served their own parish, or were not large enough.

After an exhaustive search, we finally found a beautiful church with a seating capacity of 450 that was willing to work with us. As we entered the foyer and walked into the beautiful, newly renovated sanctuary, we both knew instantly that we had found the perfect place for Leslie's service. Thrilled with our *"seek and you will find"* experience, Morti and I spontaneously looked at each other, did a high-five and said, *"YES!"*

As I entered the church the day of her service, I was thrilled to see how her friends had ensured that everything in the place reflected Leslie.

The front and back of the sanctuary were banked with Leslie's favorite flowers, which were all tastefully arranged as she would have liked them. At the front wall of the sanctuary, there was a large monitor showing a large picture of Leslie smiling down on everyone who entered there.

Three tables in the back of the room were spilling over with brochures with a picture of Leslie wearing one of her BELIEVE shirts on the cover. Over her picture were the words: Celebrating the Life of Leslie Petrone, August 15, 1961-October 11, 2011.

I picked up a brochure and, when my eyes met Leslie's, I just stood there staring at her as if frozen in time. And when I opened the brochure and my eyes fell upon the poem inside, I lost it!

### Her Journey's Just Begun

Don't think of her as gone away
her journey's just begun
life holds so many facets
this earth is only one.

Just think of her as resting
from the sorrows and the tears
in a place of warmth and comfort
where there are no days or years.

Think of how she must be wishing
that we could know her today
how nothing but our sadness
can really pass away.

And think of her as living
in the hearts of those she touched
for nothing loved is ever lost
and she was loved so much.

E. Brenneman

Instead of bringing me some measure of comfort, those heart-wrenching words, deepened my sadness. Feeling like there was a burning hot rock in my gut, I ran out of the sanctuary and headed for the restroom in the lobby.

The restroom was overflowing with women talking about Leslie, and the first one who spotted me was quick to give me her condolences. I thanked her graciously but, incapable of socializing at that moment, I retreated to a small stall at the far end of the room.

Leaning against the door of that tiny bathroom stall, still holding the brochure with Leslie's picture in my hand, I felt like my heart was breaking into a million pieces. After twenty minutes of quiet, but uncontrollable sobbing, I was feeling so emotionally raw that I found myself talking to her spirit.

*"Leslie Honey," I whispered, "just as your dad warned me would happen, I'm falling apart. Please help me calm down. I know I'm your favorite minister, but I can't do this without your help."*

Caught up in a whirlwind of emotions, I noticed that the room outside the stall had quieted down. As I pictured all those women scrambling for empty seats in a crowded sanctuary, I realized that I had little time left to pull myself together.

So, in a state of quiet desperation, I started calling on my girl again. *"Leslie Honey,"* I said, *"Please, please help me to control my emotions so that I can do what I signed up to do. I just can't do it without your help."*

Fortunately for me, that second attempt to connect with Leslie's spirit did bring a small measure of comfort to my aching heart. Soon, I was able to compose myself enough to step out of that small stall, into the larger space.

All the women who had been there previously, were now in the sanctuary waiting for the service to begin. It felt good to have some privacy even if just for a few minutes.

I walked over to the large mirror that hung above the two stainless steel sinks. And when I saw my swollen eyes, I gasped! Hoping to lessen the swelling, I splashed cold water on my face. Then I grabbed a paper towel from the dispenser, wet it with cold water and gently held it under each eye for a few minutes.

Realizing I was running out of time, I began a frantic search in my purse for some lipstick. As I applied lipstick to my parched lips, I found myself reminiscing about how Leslie, who always wanted me to look good, would remind me to do that. Even as a little girl heading to a teacher's conference with me, she would sweetly suggest, *"Put some lipstick on mommy."*

Remembering Leslie's childhood had me smiling into the mirror. Totally caught up in those life-altering, precious memories that will always live in my heart, I connected with her spirit again. And this time, she responded to my call for help.

As I stood there smiling into the mirror, a strong feeling of peace began to sweep over me. And as it enveloped me, I noticed that the "hot rock" in my gut had all but disappeared. And the intense emotional pain that I had felt just minutes earlier, had subsided considerably.

Feeling unbelievably calm, centered and poised, I combed my hair, covered my swollen eyes with a pair of eyeglasses, and walked out of that restroom into the sanctuary to officiate at Leslie's celebration of life.

Because all of Leslie's medical records listed her as Leslie Petrone, she had never used Morti's last name. In honor of Bill Hopkins and his family who had always loved her unconditionally, I included his last name in my opening words. *"Good afternoon! I'm Reverend Julie Johnson. I Stand before you because it was Leslie's wish that I officiate at her service. Therefore, as difficult as it may seem, I will be fully present for my girl whose Spirit is here with us now. So, I welcome you here today not only to reaffirm your faith in eternal life, but to remember and to celebrate the life of my wonderful daughter,* **Leslie Petrone-Hopkins** *when she last walked among us."*

As an intense feeling of love seemed to envelope the room at her celebration of life service, it was clear to all of us there how much Leslie was loved. Yet, never in our wildest dreams, could any of us have imagined how beautifully she would color the world of those whose life she had touched.

With standing room only, five hundred family members, friends, and many who were unknown to us, but had been inspired by Leslie's life, joined our family for her service. One woman, whose nineteen-year-old son had cystic fibrosis, was so inspired by Leslie's story that she had flown from New York City to San Diego just to be at her service.

Leslie didn't have the luxury of taking life for granted. Living with the awareness that life was finite, she struggled with the question, "what if there isn't going to be a next year?" Yet, despite that haunting question, she managed to live her life fully, without reservation. There is no doubt in my mind that it was Morti's devotion, her family's unconditional love, her determination to find a cure for CF, and the acceptance she received from her friends that kept her here for fifty years.

In the movie, Fried Green Tomatoes, two characters named Ruth and Izzy, are good friends who have been through all kinds of struggles together. After many wonderful years, Ruth is dying of cancer and Izzy is heart broken. Trying to comfort Ruth's little boy, Izzy says to him, *there are angels in this world that go around masquerading as people, and your mother was one of them."*

Like the character Ruth in that movie, Leslie was one of those masquerading angels constantly changing her world by bringing out the best in others. Masquerading as a daughter, a sister, a wife, and a sister-in-law, she became the glue that kept our family together. Masquerading as a family member, a friend and fund- raiser, she touched us all in the most meaningful moments of her life on this plane of existence.

That evening, when I returned home, I received this email from a couple who had been there. *"My husband and I had the blessing of attending Leslie's celebration of life today. Driving home, we realized we had been forever changed through the experience. The love in that room was pouring out and blanketing everyone.*

*Sitting or standing, we all got sticky with the sweetness of it all, and it reminded us that one person can indeed change the world."*

*"Perhaps they are not stars but rather openings in Heaven where our loved ones shine down to let us know they are happy."*

~An Eskimo Legend~

# CHAPTER 30

Losing my precious daughter had left a huge, gaping hole in my life that had turned beautiful San Diego into a nightmare of sad memories. Every corner I turned led me to a place where Leslie and I had been together. I felt her presence in my favorite restaurants, I felt her absence in my home, in my church, and on every street where we had once stood. And, I felt her presence on the beach, where we had taken my dog Lexie so many times before.

One day shortly after Leslie's passing, I got a call from a friend who was the senior minister of a large church in Florida. Nancy, who clearly understood my pain because she had lost a son about Leslie's age a few years earlier, was calling to give me her sincere condolences.

After we talked for a while, she asked if I had made any future-plans. When I shared my feelings about San Diego, she told me about a ministry in Hilton Head, South Carolina, that was in the middle of a senior-minister search.

As much as I hated to leave my precious sons and grandchildren in San Diego, deep in my heart I knew that, in order to get through the excruciating pain of losing Leslie, I needed a new environment, a different job, a complete change of scenery.

I researched the area and discovered that except for the weather and the bugs, Hilton Head, South Carolina, was as beautiful as San Diego. So, I sent a resume and received an invitation to fly out and audition. And I was hired.

My beautiful dog Lexie and I, who had exchanged the Pacific Ocean for the Atlantic, had been in South Carolina for three weeks before we found our new home. We had just moved in when Leslie appeared.

It was Saturday, March 31st, The day before my first Sunday at Unity of Hilton Head, and I was feeling very homesick. On Thursday of that week, while unpacking, I noticed that I had a sore throat. Thinking that I was simply reacting to being homesick, I ignored it.

By Saturday, I had developed a serious cough, a headache, a backache, and a temperature of 101. Needless to say, I felt extremely anxious about having flu symptoms the day before I was to make my first appearance as the new minister of Unity of Hilton Head.

So, knowing that the mind of peace always precedes healing. I sat in a comfortable chair and began affirming one of my favorite passages from A Course in Miracles: *"The peace of God is all I want."*

Enjoying the warm sunlight that was streaming through the closed window, I kept affirming "The peace of God is all I want." I had said the affirmation about three times, when suddenly, as if out of nowhere, Leslie stood in front of me and looking directly into my eyes, said, *"Hello, Mother!"*

It felt so natural to have her in my bedroom, and I was so impressed with how strong and perfectly clear her voice was, that I never questioned her presence in my room, or wondered what she was doing there. Besides that, I didn't even notice that she said, *"Hello mother!"* instead of her usual *"Hi mom."*

Thrilled to the bone to see her again, I simply replied, *"Hi, Leslie Honey!"*

Leslie not only looked beautiful, but she looked healthy and strong, just as she had looked before she had gotten so sick. Although, at the time, I remember that she was properly dressed. I was so focused on how healthy and strong she looked, that I didn't notice what she was wearing.

As she stood before me, I noticed that her eyes sparkled as they always had. Her shiny, long, black hair was draped over her shoulders, and her presence was so overpowering that I didn't remember that she was no longer alive.

Before I could utter a single word, she smiled and said, *"Mom, I'm very glad that you and Lexie are here."* And just as suddenly as she had appeared, she vanished.

*"Wait, wait, don't go"* I cried. As the words *"wait, wait don't go"* left my lips, I suddenly remembered that Leslie had died on October 11, 2011, and this was March 31, 2012.

There were so many things I wanted to ask her. For starters, I wanted to ask, *"What is it like in the world of Spirit? Have you seen grandma Josie or your Uncle Victor yet?"* I thought of so many more things I wanted to know about her new experience in living, but she was gone in a **flash!** And all those seemingly pertinent questions remained unanswered.

Yet, instead of feeling sad and disappointed that she had left me with so many unanswered questions, I felt overwhelmingly happy, content, and peaceful. In fact, it seemed as if all the stress and much of the grief and anxiety of the last five months had been instantly lifted.

Trying to indelibly mark this moment in my mind, I looked up at the clock on my wall and noticed that it was 7:00 PM. I grabbed my Diary and began writing:

*"At 7:00 PM, on Saturday, March 31, 2012, the day before my first appearance at Unity of Hilton Head as their senior minister, I had been feeling very sick when my daughter Leslie appeared in my bedroom.............."*

I don't remember how long I sat there in amazement trying to understand exactly what had just happened. What I do remember is that, I sat there for hours, writing and staring out the window through which she had come. And, when I finally got up from that chair and climbed into bed, I fell asleep immediately and slept soundly through the entire night.

When I awoke on Sunday morning, my temperature was normal, my head no longer hurt, my sore throat and cough were gone. Feeling whole and complete on April 1, 2012, I led the Sunday Service at the Unity Church of Hilton Head for the first time. In fact, I felt so well physically and so spirited, that I started my lesson with a very credible, April Fool's joke.

Leslie never appeared to me like that again. Although she has been there in my dreams, I have missed her amazing, loving, one-of-a-kind, physical presence. Since I am convinced that her Light, Grace and Courage can never be extinguished, it is easy for me to imagine Leslie breathing again and bringing her LIGHT to a far more vast dimension of Being.

Therefore, although I was deeply moved by all the meaningful cards that arrived after Leslie's passing. The one that made my heart leap with joy simply said, ***"She's Breathing!"***

*"Some journeys take us far from home. Some adventures lead us to our destiny."*

~ *C.S. Lewis~*

# EPILOGUE

One week after Leslie's passing, keeping my promise that I would write about our journey through the world of cystic fibrosis, and intent that her amazing life would never be forgotten, I attempted to write this book. However, the agonizing pain in the pit of my stomach, as well as the need to make sense of my own life in the wake of Leslie's death, extended the writing process to seven years.

However, I needn't have to worry about Leslie's legacy. A few weeks after her Celebration of Life service, I received a phone call from the directors of the San Diego chapter of the Cystic Fibrosis Foundation asking if they could meet with me in my home. As it turned out, they had come to assure me that whether I could write this book or not, Leslie would never be forgotten.

The good news they brought that day was that the name of the annual "Women Who Take Your Breath Away" award, given to an extraordinary woman living with the disease, of which Leslie had been a recipient, would now be permanently changed to: **The Leslie Petrone, Women Who Take Your Breath Away Award.**

Elated and grateful, I couldn't but believe that the good that I had been seeking, was also seeking me.

# ACKNOWLEDGEMENTS

This book is dedicated to:
Leslie's husband Bill Hopkins, known to his
friends as Morti, whose love and devotion gave
her the emotional stability and determination to
Keep-on-Keeping-on.

Her brothers, Russ, Tom, Eric who loved her
unconditionally and mirrored wholeness to her.

Her dear friend Stacy Motenko-
Carbona who raised $150,000.00 for
a cure six months after her death.

To her family and caring friends who loved
her and were always there for her.

Printed in the United States
by Baker & Taylor Publisher Services